A Note From Rick Renner

I am on a personal quest to see a "revival of the Bible" so people can establish their lives on a firm foundation that will stand strong and endure the test as end-time storm winds begin to intensify.

In order to experience a revival of the Bible in your personal life, it is important to take time each day to read, receive, and apply its truths to your life. James tells us that if we will continue in the perfect law of liberty — refusing to be forgetful hearers, but determined to be doers — we will be blessed in our ways. As you watch or listen to the programs in this series and work through this corresponding study guide, I trust you will search the Scriptures and allow the Holy Spirit to help you hear something new from God's Word that applies specifically to your life. I encourage you to be a doer of the Word He reveals to you. Whatever the cost, I assure you — it will be worth it.

> Thy words were found, and I did eat them;
> and thy word was unto me the joy and rejoicing of mine heart:
> for I am called by thy name, O Lord God of hosts.
> —Jeremiah 15:16

Your brother and friend in Jesus Christ,

Rick Renner

Rick Renner

Dream Thieves
Overcoming Obstacles to Fulfill Your Dreams

Copyright © 2022 by Rick Renner
1814 W. Tacoma St.
Broken Arrow, OK 74012

Published by Rick Renner Ministries
www.renner.org

ISBN 13: 978-1-6675-0258-8

eBook ISBN 13: 978-1-6675-0259-5

How To Use This Study Guide

This ten-lesson study guide corresponds to *"Dream Thieves" With Rick Renner* (Renner TV). Each lesson in this study guide covers a topic that is addressed during the program series, with questions and references supplied to draw you deeper into your own private study of the Scriptures on this subject.

To derive the most benefit from this study guide, consider the following:

First, watch or listen to the program prior to working through the corresponding lesson in this guide. (Programs can also be viewed at **renner.org** by clicking on the Media/Archives links or on our Renner Ministries YouTube channel.)

Second, take the time to look up the scriptures included in each lesson. Prayerfully consider their application to your own life.

Third, use a journal or notebook to make note of your answers to each lesson's Study Questions and Practical Application challenges.

Fourth, invest specific time in prayer and in the Word of God to consult with the Holy Spirit. Write down the scriptures or insights He reveals to you.

Finally, take action! Whatever the Lord tells you to do according to His Word, do it.

For added insights on this subject, it is recommended that you obtain Rick Renner's book *Dream Thieves: Overcoming Obstacles To Fulfill Your Dreams.* You may also select from Rick's other available resources by placing your order at **renner.org** or by calling 1-800-742-5593.

TOPIC

Holding Fast to Your Word From God

SCRIPTURES

1. **Ephesians 1:4** — According as he hath chosen us in him before the foundation of the world....

2. **Luke 14:28-30** — For which of you, intending to build a tower, sitteth not down first, and counteth the cost, whether he have sufficient to finish it? Lest haply, after he hath laid the foundation, and is not able to finish it, all that behold it begin to mock him, saying, This man began to build, and was not able to finish.

3. **Hebrews 10:23** — Let us hold fast the profession of our faith without wavering; (for he is faithful that promised).

4. **Romans 1:18** — For the wrath of God is revealed from heaven against all ungodliness and unrighteousness of men, who hold the truth in unrighteousness.

GREEK WORDS

1. "chosen" — ἐκλέγομαι (*eklegomai*): to call out, choose, elect, or select; used to refer to individuals who were selected for a specific purpose; conveys the idea of the privilege and honor of being chosen; it is so connected to the idea of privilege that those being selected should look upon themselves as honored, esteemed, and respected

2. "before" — πρό (*pro*): before, in advance

3. "foundation" — καταβολή (*katabole*): a compound of κατα (*kata*) and βάλλω (*ballo*); the preposition κατα (*kata*) means down, and βάλλω (*ballo*) means "I throw" or "I hurl"; pictures an act that occurred long before or in advance of when the first layers of the universe were hurled into place by God's spoken Word

4. "hold fast" — κατέχω (*katecho*): a compound of κατα (*kata*) and ἔχω (*echo*); the preposition κατα (*kata*) carries the idea of something that comes downward or something that comes down so hard and heavily that it is overpowering, dominating, and even subjugating, thus, something that conquers, subdues, and immediately begins to demonstrate

its overwhelming, influencing power; the word ἔχω (*echo*) means "I have" and carries the idea of possession; when compounded, the word doesn't just mean to embrace, it actually means to embrace something tightly, and because of the preposition *kata*, it is the image of someone who finds the object of his dreams and then holds it down — even to the point of sitting on it — in order to dominate and take control of it; to suppress

5. "hold" — κατέχω (*katecho*): to suppress, lest it get out and positively change the way people think and believe

SYNOPSIS

The ten lessons in this study on *Dream Thieves* will focus on the following topics:

- Holding Fast to Your Word From God
- Four Dream Thieves You Must Overcome
- Coming Into Divine Alignment
- Do Not Give Up on Your Faith
- The Behavior of Real Faith
- Sustaining the Fire in Your Heart
- Faith and Patience: A Marriage That Produces Results
- Taking Steps To Fulfill Your Dream
- A Threefold Cord Is Not Easily Broken
- The Consequences of Surrender

The emphasis of this lesson:

Everyone has been selected by God to fulfill a specific purpose on the earth. The dream He plants in each of our hearts is uniquely tailored to who we are, and in order to see that dream become reality, we must learn how to fight against the debilitating dream thieves that press against our souls.

Has God spoken to your heart and given you a dream of something He wants you to do for Him? Does it seem like an impossible task to accomplish? Have you been hindered by obstacles that seem to come out of nowhere and harass your progress? You are not alone.

Rick and Denise Renner were given a dream to move to the former Soviet Union, and in the process of coming to grips with this new direction for their lives, they had many unanswered questions and challenges that blocked their way. Rick calls these obstacles *dream thieves*, and in this lesson and those that follow, he shares biblical truths he learned that will help you push past all the doubts and fears that are keeping you from fulfilling God's calling.

God Handpicked You Before the Foundation of the World

There is no one else like you anywhere on earth. When you were created, God gave you fingerprints, an eye pattern, a voice, and a chemistry that is uniquely yours. In the same way, He has also gifted you with specific talents and skills to accomplish an assignment that only you can fulfill. The Bible says, "Each person is given something to do that shows who God is: Everyone gets in on it, everyone benefits" (1 Corinthians 12:7 *MSG*).

What makes this truth even more profound is that God had His hands on your life even before you were born! Ephesians 1:4 tells us, "According as he hath chosen us in him before the foundation of the world...." The word "chosen" in this verse is the Greek word *eklegomai*, a compound of the word *ek*, which means *out*, and the word *legomai*, which means *I say*. When these words are compounded, the new word *eklegomai* means *to call out, choose, elect,* or *select*. It was used to refer to individuals who were selected for a specific purpose. In fact, it was the very word used to describe men who were chosen to serve in the military.

Moreover, the word *eklegomai* conveys the idea of *the privilege and honor of being chosen*. It is so connected to the idea of privilege that those being selected should look upon themselves as *honored, esteemed,* and *respected*. So rather than badger yourself and say you're not worth anything, say what God says. Say, "I've been personally chosen by God. He brought me into the world, and I'm such a privileged individual." You need to esteem who you are because God has esteemed you. And He did it "before the foundation of the world" (Ephesians 1:4).

The word "before" in the verse is the Greek word *pro*, which means *long in advance of*. According to this verse, God already knew you and had selected you long in advance before the foundation of the world was ever put in place.

This brings us to the word "foundation" — the Greek word *katabole*. It is a compound of the preposition *kata*, meaning *down*, and the word *ballo*, which means *"I throw"* or *"I hurl."* When *kata* and *ballo* form *katabole*, it pictures *an act that occurred long before or in advance of when the first layers of the universe were hurled into place by God's spoken Word.* That's how long God has been waiting for you to be birthed on the earth and fulfill your destiny. Friend, you are not an afterthought!

It's Normal To Have Questions

Now many of us have a good idea of God's calling on our lives and have started out passionately pursuing our purpose. But because the fulfillment of our dream has dragged on and on, the fire in our heart has dwindled to a mere flicker. Tragically, we haven't learned how to navigate the hindering, dream-destroying forces that attack our mind, our will, and our emotions. Consequently, we retreat from what God has revealed to us and simply watch life pass by.

Nothing is more tragic than this: that a person would let go of his or her dream — the very purpose for which he or she was born into this world.

Indeed, when you lift your foot and begin to step forward to obey the Lord, every part of your soul will scream out and say, "What if you're making a mistake? What if this doesn't work? What will people say? You will have gotten yourself into a mess, and then what will you do?"

Although many people try to ignore or even deny the existence of these kinds of questions, they are a normal part of the process of a person who is thinking about doing something new in his or her life. Instead of hiding from or ignoring the questions, begin to search out and pray for answers.

Prayerfully seek God's wisdom as you look at every question, as you face every fear, and as you examine every doubt. Be totally honest with yourself and God and don't stop seeking Him until you've heard from Him, and He has equipped you with the answers you need to decide what you're going to do.

Count the Cost

There's nothing wrong with taking a real good look at the new endeavor that is before you. As a matter of fact, Jesus recommends you *count the cost* before tackling a new task. In Luke 14:28-30, He said:

For which of you, intending to build a tower, sitteth not down first, and counteth the cost, whether he have sufficient to finish it? Lest haply, after he hath laid the foundation, and is not able to finish it, all that behold it begin to mock him, saying, This man began to build, and was not able to finish.

The reason many people fail is not for lack of vision, but for lack of resolve — and resolve is born out of *counting the cost*! The truth is, it's easy to start a project, but finishing it is something different altogether. That is where resolve comes in. This God-empowered determination, tenacity, and steadfastness come out of surrendering yourself to Him and looking at the project from all angles. Believe it or not, considering the challenges that could present themselves reduces the shocks, surprises, and stress that often arise on the path to completion.

What's interesting is that the Holy Spirit will use questions, doubts, and fears you may have to incite you to count the cost before pursuing the dream God has put in your heart. For this reason, those questions and doubts are valid and should be dealt with before you make any big change in your life. This process of evaluation isn't to promote doubt and fear. Instead, it's an important step to help you develop an inner resolve that will endure, regardless of any obstacles or difficulties you may encounter.

The fact is your new course of action will be challenged. Whether you are starting a new career, opening a new business, launching into a new ministry, or taking your family in a new direction, you will likely encounter difficulties you've never experienced before. Therefore, instead of being blindsided by what could happen, count the cost and think things through from the beginning.

Pursuing Your Dream Requires Great Stretching

Rick shared how many years ago when he and Denise were serving as pastors in a very small church in Arkansas, God spoke to him and said, "Rick, it's time for you to step into the next phase of your life and begin a national teaching ministry in the United States." As you can imagine, he was challenged to the core, and many questions began to swirl in his head.

How am I going to do that? he thought. *I've been pastoring a tiny church in Arkansas, far removed from the mainstream of ministry. I have no contacts beyond our little church, and very few people know me. How in the world are doors going to open for me to begin my teaching ministry?*

For Rick and Denise to wholeheartedly step out in faith, they prayerfully examined the new endeavor to which God was calling them. They prayed diligently about all their questions and thought about the possible challenges and hurdles they would face. They also sought godly counsel from trusted friends, and in the end concluded that launching into a teaching ministry was indeed God's plan. They then stepped out with the full knowledge of what was before them.

The next major stretching Rick experienced was when the Lord told him to begin writing books. *Write books?* He thought. *I'm an unknown author. What are the chances that my books would be blessed and bought?* Again, the questions swirled in his mind, so he took them to the Lord in prayer and began to seek wisdom from his pastor and other trusted leaders. Once he understood what he was facing and knew God had spoken to him, he launched out and began writing.

Then came the most difficult stretching of all — when God told Rick to move his entire family to the Soviet Union. There were so many things for him and Denise to think about before they made such a move. Again, questions abounded, and the naysayers were saying, "Where are you going to get the money to live? How are you going to support your ministry in the states and in the Soviet Union simultaneously? What if you get over there and that part of the world erupts into turmoil? What are you and your children going to do if you get caught in the middle of a big mess like that? What's going to happen to you?"

All those questions were good, legitimate concerns that needed to be considered. Rick and Denise couldn't just charge ahead without much prayer and carefully thinking through these potential challenges. Now more than ever, they needed the Spirit-stamped confirmation in their hearts that it was God who was calling them to take such a strong leap of faith, and that is exactly what they received.

What Do You Do Once God's Calling Is Confirmed?

Once your questions and concerns have been addressed and God's calling has been confirmed, your next step is to set your heart on the assignment and hold onto it with all your might. Essentially, that is what God tells us in Hebrews 10:23:

> **Let us hold fast the profession of our faith without wavering; (for he is faithful that promised).**

The words "hold fast" in this verse are very important. They are a translation of the Greek word *katecho*, which is a compound of the words *kata* and *echo*. The preposition *kata* carries the idea of *something that comes downward* or *something that comes down so hard and heavily it is overpowering, dominating, and even subjugating*. Thus, it is *something that conquers, subdues, and immediately begins to demonstrate its overwhelming, influencing power*.

The second part of the word — *echo* — means "I have" and carries the idea of *possession*. When compounded, the new word *katecho* doesn't just mean to embrace, it actually means *to embrace something tightly*, and because of the inclusion of the preposition *kata*, it is the image of *someone who finds the object of his dreams and then holds it down* — even to the point of sitting on it — *in order to dominate and take control of it*.

What is interesting about this word *katecho* is that it can also be used negatively, which is what we see in Romans 1:18, which says, "For the wrath of God is revealed from heaven against all ungodliness and unrighteousness of men, who hold the truth in unrighteousness." The word "hold" in this verse is *katecho*, the same word translated as "hold fast" in Hebrews 10:23. In this case it describes wicked men who are *holding back* and *suppressing* the truth, lest it gets out and positively changes the way people think and believe.

Friend, when the dream thieves come to try to talk you out of your God-given dream, you've got to wrap your arms around it, sit on top of it, and don't let anyone pull it away from you. That's what it means to "hold fast the profession of your faith."

In our next lesson, we will examine four primary dream thieves that come to try to take away our dream or word from God. These include *time*, *Satan*, your *friends*, and your *family*.

STUDY QUESTIONS

Study to shew thyself approved unto God, a workman that needeth not to be ashamed, rightly dividing the word of truth.
— 2 Timothy 2:15

1. In order for you to know and understand your purpose, you need to be able to hear God speaking to you. What does Jesus say about hearing

His voice in John 10:3-5,14 and 27? According to Second Timothy 3:15-17 and Hebrews 4:12, what does God use regularly to speak to you and direct your life? What adjustments can you make in your daily routine to tap into this amazing treasury of divine wisdom on a more regular basis?

2. Ephesians 1:4 says that God chose you *before* the foundation of the world and that He highly esteems you. How does Ephesians 2:1-10 reiterate and expand on this powerful truth? How does having this understanding affect the way you see yourself?

PRACTICAL APPLICATION

> But be ye doers of the word, and not hearers only,
> deceiving your own selves.
> —James 1:22

1. Has God spoken to your heart and given you a dream regarding something He wants you to do for Him? If so, what is it? Is there anything about the dream that seems like an impossible task to accomplish?

2. Take some time to "count the cost" of the new endeavor, writing down the questions, doubts, and fears you're facing. Bring these to the Lord in prayer and begin to search for the answers you need from Him and from trusted friends and sources.

LESSON 2

TOPIC

Four Dream Thieves You Must Overcome

SCRIPTURES

1. **Ephesians 1:4** — According as he hath chosen us in him before the foundation of the world....

2. **Hebrews 10:23** — Let us hold fast the profession of our faith without wavering; (for he is faithful that promised).

3. **Romans 1:18** — For the wrath of God is revealed from heaven against all ungodliness and unrighteousness of men, who hold the truth in unrighteousness.

4. **1 Peter 5:6** — Humble yourselves therefore under the mighty hand of God, that he may exalt you in due time.

5. **Ephesians 1:11** — In whom also we have obtained an inheritance, being predestinated according to the purpose of him who worketh all things after the counsel of his own will.

6. **Ephesians 2:10** (*NKJV*) — For we are His workmanship, created in Christ Jesus for good works, which God prepared beforehand that we should walk in them.

7. **Psalm 139:16-18** (*NIV*) — Your eyes saw my unformed body; all the days ordained for me were written in your book before one of them came to be. How precious to me are your thoughts, God! How vast is the sum of them! Were I to count them, they would outnumber the grains of sand — when I awake, I am still with you.

8. **Jeremiah 1:4,5** — Then the word of the Lord came unto me, saying, before I formed thee in the belly I knew thee; and before thou camest forth out of the womb I sanctified thee, and I ordained thee a prophet unto the nations.

9. **Galatians 1:15,16** — But when it pleased God, who separated me from my mother's womb, and called me by his grace, to reveal his Son in me, that I might preach him among the heathen; immediately I conferred not with flesh and blood.

GREEK WORDS

1. "chosen" — ἐκλέγομαι (*eklegomai*): to call out, choose, elect, or select; used to refer to individuals who were selected for a specific purpose; conveys the idea of the privilege and honor of being chosen; it is so connected to the idea of privilege that those being selected should look upon themselves as honored, esteemed, and respected

2. "before" — πρό (*pro*): before, in advance

3. "foundation" — καταβολή (*katabole*): a compound of κατα (*kata*) and βάλλω (*ballo*); the preposition κατα (*kata*) means down, and βάλλω (*ballo*) means "I throw" or "I hurl"; pictures an act that occurred long before or in advance of when the first layers of the universe were hurled into place by God's spoken Word

4. "hold fast" — **κατέχω** (*katecho*): a compound of **κατα** (*kata*) and **ἔχω** (*echo*); the preposition **κατα** (*kata*) carries the idea of something that comes downward or something that comes down so hard and heavily that it is overpowering, dominating, and even subjugating, thus, something that conquers, subdues, and immediately begins to demonstrate its overwhelming, influencing power; the word **ἔχω** (*echo*) means "I have" and carries the idea of possession; when compounded, the word doesn't just mean to embrace, it actually means to embrace something tightly, and because of the preposition *kata*, it is the image of someone who finds the object of his dreams and then holds it down — even to the point of sitting on it — in order to dominate and take control of it; to suppress

5. "hold" — **κατέχω** (*katecho*): to suppress, lest it get out and positively change the way people think and believe

SYNOPSIS

When you finally begin to see God's will for your life coming into focus, His plan begins to awaken in your heart, and you come to understand what job to take, what business to start, what ministry He's called you to fulfill, and so forth. But if you don't hold fast to that God-given vision, tightly embracing what He has shown you, the dream thieves will see to it that you slowly let your dream slip away from you.

That is why we're told in Scripture to "hold fast" to what God has spoken to our hearts, which means we must seize our dream — wrap our arms of faith around it, hold it down, grasp it tightly, and place all our weight on top of it. If we don't, the dream thieves of life will come to rob us of the wonderful plan God has for us. If they succeed in doing so, they will steal our uniqueness and our individual purpose in the magnificent plan of God — and nothing could be more tragic than that.

The emphasis of this lesson:

There are several different dream thieves that try to steal God's vision and purpose for our lives. The four primary ones that all of us will face are time, Satan, the voice of friends, and the voice of family.

You've Been 'Chosen' by God

Before time began, God had YOU on His mind! Ephesians 1:4 declares, "According as he hath chosen us in him before the foundation of the world...." In our first lesson, we saw that the word "chosen" is a translation of the Greek word *eklegomai*, which literally means *to call out, to choose, to elect,* or *to select*. It conveys the idea of the privilege and honor of being chosen. The use of this word tells us that God chose us, selected us, and elected us on purpose — and He did it "before the foundation of the world."

The word "before" in Greek is *pro*, meaning *before* or *in advance*. And the Greek word used here for "foundation" is *katabole*, a compound of the words *kata* and *ballo*. The preposition *kata* means *down*, and *ballo* means *to throw* or *to hurl*. When *kata* and *ballo* are joined to form *katabole* — translated here as "foundation" — it signifies that long before or in advance of when the first layers of the universe were hurled into place by God's spoken Word, He was thinking of you and had chosen you to be a part of His family.

Taking into account the original Greek meaning, here is the *Renner Interpretive Version (RIV)* of Ephesians 1:4:

> **...Even before the first layer of the universe was hurled into place, God was peering into the future to see whom He would choose — and He saw us there! When He saw us, He spoke and said, "Out!" And when He said those words, He literally "selected" us as His own....**

Friend, you are not an accident or an afterthought. You are a handpicked vital part of God's plan. He selected you before time began and has set aside a divine assignment that only you can carry out.

'Hold Fast' to God's Plan for Your Life

For you to fulfill the dream God has planted in your heart, it's imperative that you understand the meaning of Hebrews 10:23. It says, "Let us hold fast the profession of our faith without wavering; (for he is faithful that promised)." We learned in Lesson 1 that the Greek word for "hold fast" is *katecho*, and it is a compound of the words *kata* and *echo*. The preposition *kata* carries the idea of *something that comes downward* or *something that comes down so hard and heavily that it is overpowering, dominating,* and even *subjugating.*

The word *echo* means *"I have," "I hold,"* or *"I possess."* When *kata* and *echo* are compounded, the new word *katecho* means *to embrace something tightly,* and because the preposition *kata* is included, it is the image of someone who finds the object of his dreams and then holds it down — even to the point of sitting on it — in order to dominate and take control of it. Regardless of what comes against him, this person is not letting go of the treasure he has finally found and made his own.

Interestingly, the word *katecho* is also used in Romans 1:18, but in a negative sense. The verse says, "For the wrath of God is revealed from heaven against all ungodliness and unrighteousness of men, who hold the truth in unrighteousness." In this passage, the word "hold" is the Greek word *katecho*, and Paul uses it to describe wicked men who *suppress* the truth. Clearly, these individuals know what the truth is, but they don't like it! Therefore, they "put a lid on" it, lest it get out and positively change the way people think and believe.

A modern-day example of *katecho* is when the gatekeepers in the media are told to "sit on a story" rather than publish it because highly influential people don't want the truth to be told so that it gets away from their ability to control it. It is this same word — *katecho* — that is used in Hebrews 10:23 to urge us to "hold fast" to God's will for our lives. He wants us to embrace it tightly, hold it down, and take dominating control of it so that it cannot in any way get away from us.

FOUR PRIMARY DREAM THIEVES

DREAM THIEF #1: TIME

In and of itself, *time* is a neutral force. It can work for us or against us; it can be a healing or a destructive force. You will face several dream thieves in life, but *time* is one of the primary strategies Satan uses to try to steal your dreams. There's just something about the passage of time that has a way of gnawing away at your faith and perseverance.

As the weeks, months, and years pass and your dreams remain unfulfilled, the enemy will use the passage of time to bring accusations against your mind. He'll begin to whisper, *You're nothing more than a dreamer! You probably didn't receive a true word from the Lord after all. It was just something you wanted to happen — a wild idea you dreamed up to make you feel more important in your small, insignificant world! You're just a dreamer. So let go of that fantasy and get back to the real world.*

Perhaps it seems like your entire life has been put "on hold" since the moment the dream was first birthed in your heart. You may even have other desires in your heart. You could have gone on with your life and done other things. Instead, you just camped out and are now waiting for the dream to come to pass, but since it hasn't come to pass, all you can see is the time you've wasted.

Only God knows how many men and women of faith have come to this place in their spiritual walk. Having waited so long to see their victory, they regret that God ever spoke to them. Instead of holding tightly to their dream with greater effort and resolve, the passing of time pressures them to let it slip right through their fingers. Finally, these believers abandon God's plan altogether. Sadly, they often let go of their dream just as they are on the brink of experiencing the full manifestation of His promise in their lives.

First Peter 5:6 instructs us, "Humble yourselves therefore under the mighty hand of God, that he may exalt you *in due time.*" Whenever time becomes a dream thief that attempts to steal our God-given vision, we must "hold fast" and remind ourselves again and again that it *will* come to pass "in due time."

Furthermore, we have to establish our hearts in the Word of God, refusing to be moved or shaken by the length of time it takes for us to see the fruit of our labor and the manifestation of our steadfast faith. Instead, look time in the eye and say, "I'm camping out right here on what God has told me until I see the manifestation."

DREAM THIEF #2: SATAN

Dream thief number two is *Satan* himself. If you get beyond the dream thief of time, you will most certainly begin to hear the sarcastic, condemning voice of the serpent ringing in your ears. He will come along and accuse you of being just another run-of-the-mill, ordinary person who's tired of the status quo and doesn't like the direction his or her life has taken. He'll try to convince you that you're living in a made-up fantasy world to cope with your disappointing life.

The devil knows the strategic value of convincing you that the dream for greatness that God has placed in your heart is nothing more than a self-exalting ego trip. If you listen to him, he'll convince you that you were not brought into this world for anything special. Remember what Jesus called him — the thief that comes only to steal, kill, and destroy (*see* John 10:10).

To effectively fight against and demolish the devil's lies, you have to look to the Word of God for specific truths. Scripture will give you strength and build your steadfastness in the faith. For instance, according to Ephesians 1:4, you can tell the devil, "God handpicked me for His purposes before the first layer of the universe was ever put into place!" This is a principle seen in many places throughout Scripture, including Ephesians 1:11, which says:

> **In whom also we have obtained an inheritance, being predestinated according to the purpose of him who worketh all things after the counsel of his own will.**

Taking into account the original Greek meaning, here is the *Renner Interpretive Version (RIV)* of Ephesians 1:11:

> **...Before anything existed, God chose us! God devised every step to bring us to this place, and God has executed every single step of the plan that He had determined by His own counsel so long ago.**

Here again, we see in this verse that you are not an afterthought! You have been in God's mind and on His heart since before creation. We see a very similar assertion in Ephesians 2:10 (*NKJV*), where the apostle Paul declares:

> **For we are His workmanship, created in Christ Jesus for good works, which God prepared beforehand that we should walk in them.**

Through David, the Holy Spirit expands this principle of God's intimate awareness of us even further. In Psalm 139:16-18 (*NIV*), David writes:

> Your eyes saw my unformed body; all the days ordained for me were written in your book before one of them came to be. How precious to me are your thoughts, God! How vast is the sum of them! Were I to count them, they would outnumber the grains of sand — when I awake, I am still with you.

Again and again, we hear from these men who lived centuries apart but were moved by the same Holy Spirit to proclaim the amazing foreknowledge of our God. We see both Jeremiah and the apostle Paul reiterate this same truth in their writings:

> Then the word of the Lord came unto me [Jeremiah], saying, before I formed thee in the belly I knew thee; and before thou camest forth out of the womb I sanctified thee, and I ordained thee a prophet unto the nations.
>
> — Jeremiah 1:4,5

> But when it pleased God, who separated me [Paul] from my mother's womb, and called me by his grace, to reveal his Son in me, that I might preach him among the heathen; immediately I conferred not with flesh and blood.
>
> — Galatians 1:15,16

Are you hearing what God is saying? Over and over, He is telling you through His Word that you are not a mistake or an accident. Just as He was aware of and had a plan for Paul, Jeremiah, David, and everyone else, He has a plan for you! And He designed that plan before He hung the stars or separated the land from the sea. So when the devil tries to tell you you're nothing special and your life has no significance, tell him to hit the road! God says otherwise, and you have His Word on it!

DREAM THIEF #3: FRIENDS

Along with the dream thieves of time and Satan, the voice of your friends can also become a major hindrance to you fulfilling your dream. Although for the most part they mean well and want to help you have a more balanced perspective of what you're about to launch out into, you need to have discernment to know who is talking and offering you advice from a fleshly perspective.

Now many of your friends who love God and are pursuing their own walk with Him will have a confirming witness in their spirits and will know that you have heard from God. They will fully support you and pray for you as you pursue your dream. But that will not be the case with everyone who is close to you.

For example, if God has told you to step out and start a new business, your friends might say: "Have you considered job security and the state of the economy? You have a guaranteed salary, medical insurance, and great benefits where you are now, so why not be content with what you have? If you launch out to start a new business, you're going to lose all that."

Although there is some logic in these questions, if you've already carefully looked at these issues and you really know the direction you're considering is what God is telling you to do, then you need to embrace it and hold fast to that dream, regardless of what your friends tell you.

The reality is that change frightens people who are looking at things from a natural perspective. In other words, those who are more focused on this temporary, earthly life will not see or understand the eternal purpose of God's plans. Likewise, if your friends think their lives are mediocre or ordinary, your quest for excellence in God will probably threaten them, and they may very well try to convince you that you're making a mistake. The bottom line: Your success in obeying God will amplify any other believer's failure to faithfully pursue God's plan for his or her life.

Those who are true, God-given friends will eventually come alongside you and say, "You know, I may not understand what you're doing, but I know that you believe you've heard from God. Instead of dragging you into my doubt and unbelief, I'm going to stand by you and support you and pray for you." That's what a real friend will do.

DREAM THIEF #4: FAMILY

The fourth common dream thief that all of us will have to deal with is the voice of our *family*. This challenge can often be the most difficult to navigate. *Time* passes and brings new seasons; the voice of the *enemy* can be rebuked and silenced with God's Word, and you can say goodbye to unsupportive *friends* who have a fleshly focus. *Family*, on the other hand, is with you for life, and it is often difficult to show them love and respect and obey God at the same time.

Think about it: Your family members have watched you grow up in the natural. They've seen you attempt to do other things in the past that were unsuccessful, and more than anyone else in the world, they know your faults and weaknesses. So when you announce that the Lord has told you to do something grand and glorious, some family members are going to remember — and remind you of — the last thing you said you were going to do that turned out to be a dismal failure. They may also try to convince you that you're compensating for your inadequacies by living in a fantasy world instead of facing your problems realistically and living as "normal people" do.

Realize that because they love and care about you deeply, they are voicing their concerns because they don't want you to go through more hurt and pain. So when they blast you with their questions and submit a series of devastating scenarios that could happen, don't be disturbed. Listen to what they have to say and sincerely thank them for their concern. When all is said and done, know that God has spoken to you and *hold fast* to what He has said.

Friend, if God has spoken a word of direction to you, these four dream thieves will likely come against you. Your job is to hold fast to the vision He has placed in your heart...

- No matter how much time it takes.

- No matter how many times you need to tell the devil he's a liar and that your old, selfish nature is dead.

- No matter how many friends tell you that your plans are crazy and then abandon you.

- No matter how deeply it hurts when family members come against your dream because of their love and concern for you.

If you really know that God is the One who placed the dream in your heart, hold fast to what He has spoken and let it take precedence over every other argument!

STUDY QUESTIONS

Study to shew thyself approved unto God, a workman that needeth not to be ashamed, rightly dividing the word of truth.
— 2 Timothy 2:15

1. It is vitally important for you to know just how much God is always aware of you. Although the devil would want you to think God has

forgotten and abandoned you, He has not — and these passages of Scripture prove it. Take some time to reflect on these powerful promises and write down what the Holy Spirit shows you about God's involvement in your life.

- **Psalm 139:1-10, 13-18**
- **Psalm 56:8**
- **Luke 12:7; Matthew 10:29-31**
- **Malachi 3:16-18**

2. Many people wonder — some even argue — as to when life actually begins. According to Jeremiah 1:4,5; Isaiah 49:1; and Psalm 139:13-16, where does life come from and when does it begin?

3. To effectively fight against the lies of the enemy and the fleshly thinking of friends and family, you have to look to the Word of God for specific truths. What go-to scriptures has the Holy Spirit helped you find that empower you to keep pursuing the dream He's placed in your heart?

PRACTICAL APPLICATION

But be ye doers of the word, and not hearers only, deceiving your own selves.
—James 1:22

1. Of the four primary dream thieves — *time, Satan, friends*, and *family* — which one have you had to fight against most often? What particular phrases (or lies) have come against your mind? How have you typically dealt with these attacks?

2. Does it seem like your entire life has been put "on hold" since the moment God deposited a dream in your heart? Have you thought about how much better your life would be right now if God had never given you that dream? What is the Holy Spirit showing you in this lesson to counter that kind of thinking and begin pursuing your dream again?

3. Your true friends will genuinely love God and have a confirming witness in their spirits and know when you have heard from Him. With that in mind, who would you say are your real friends? When do you

remember them supporting you and praying for you? What were you pursuing and believing God to do in and through your life?

TOPIC

Coming Into Divine Alignment

SCRIPTURES

1. **Hebrews 10:23** — Let us hold fast the profession of our faith without wavering; (for he is faithful that promised).

GREEK WORDS

1. "hold fast" — **κατέχω** (*katecho*): to embrace something tightly, and because of the preposition **κατα** (*kata*), it is the image of someone who finds the object of his dreams and then holds it down — even to the point of sitting on it — in order to dominate and take control of it; to suppress

SYNOPSIS

In Lesson 2, we examined four primary dream thieves that come against all of us. The first is *time*, which tries to tell you to give up because if it was going to happen, it would have happened already. The next dream thief is *Satan* himself who whispers his lies against the truth of God's Word and tells you that what you're hearing is just your imagination and that you're crazy.

If you make it beyond the dream thieves of time and Satan, the third dream thief you'll encounter is the voice of your *friends*. When they hear you share about the new direction God has given you, they will probably try to give you a more "balanced perspective" of what you'll experience if you do what you say you're going to do.

The fourth dream thief you will face is the voice of your *family*. Because they really love you and don't want you to suffer hardship, they will voice their concerns and fears — even try to talk you out of doing what you feel you're supposed to do — all with the hope of preventing you from repeating the hurt and pain of the past.

If you're going to do what God has told you to do, you'll have to be committed to *hold fast* to your dream no matter how long it takes, no matter how many times you have to tell the devil to hit the road, and no matter how many friends tell you that your plans are crazy. Likewise, no matter how much it hurts when family members come against your dream because of their love and concern for you, you have to tightly embrace the vision God has placed in your heart so firmly that nothing can steal it from you.

The emphasis of this lesson:

To confess something in faith is to say the very same thing God is saying and believe it to be true in your heart. In this condition of divine alignment, your heart and God's heart are in such agreement on an issue that they're beating in perfect syncopation. In that position, a door for God's power to flow through you opens and supernatural things begin to take place.

A Review of Our Anchor Verse

Looking again at our anchor verse in Hebrews 10:23, it says, "Let us hold fast the profession of our faith without wavering; (for he is faithful that promised)." We have noted in the previous two lessons that the words "hold fast" are a translation of the Greek word *katecho*, which is a compound of the words *kata* and *echo*. The word *kata* is a preposition describing *something that is overpowering, dominating,* and even *subjugating* — something that comes down very hard and heavy.

The second part of *katecho* is *echo*, which means *"I have," "I hold," "I possess,"* or *"I embrace."* When *kata* and *echo* are compounded to form *katecho*, it means *to embrace something so tightly that nothing or no one can take it away from you*. It is the picture of a person who finds the object of his dreams and then holds it down — even to the point of sitting on it — so that it will remain in his control.

Understand that when God has given you explicit instructions and the voice of time, Satan, friends, or family try to talk you out of it, you've got to wrap your arms around your dream, hold it down, and embrace it so tightly that it doesn't slip away.

We noted that this word *katecho* is also used in Romans 1:18, but in a negative sense. Here, Paul wrote, "For the wrath of God is revealed from heaven against all ungodliness and unrighteousness of men, who hold the truth in unrighteousness." The word "hold" is the Greek word *katecho*, and Paul used it to describe wicked men who *suppress* the truth. It is the equivalent of Paul saying, "They *put a lid on* the truth because they don't want it to get out and positively change people's lives."

Again, that same word *katecho* is what is used positively in Hebrews 10:23. When we know we have received a word from God for our lives, He wants us to embrace it tightly, hold it down, and restrain it with all our might so that it cannot be taken away from us.

What Does It Mean To 'Confess' Something in Faith?

It is important to see that the writer of Hebrews said we are to hold fast "…the profession of our faith…" (Hebrews 10:23). The word "profession" here is very important. It is the Greek word *homologia* and is sometimes translated as the word *confession*. It's actually a compound of the word *homo*, which means *of the very same kind*, and the word *logia*, which is from the word *logos*, the term for *words*. When these words are compounded to form *homologia*, it means *to say the same thing, to repeat the same thing, to be in agreement*, or *to confess*. Rather than just parroting what somebody else says, this word signifies coming into full agreement with someone else on a particular issue.

For example, take God's "Word," which is the Greek word *logos*, the second part of the word *homologia*. When you get into agreement with a specific truth in Scripture, it means you agree with God and believe what He believes, see what He sees, and understand what He understands regarding that truth. In fact, you and God are in such agreement on that issue that your heart and His heart begin to beat in perfect syncopation! Indeed, you and God have come into divine alignment on that subject.

Jesus referred to the principle of divine alignment in Mark 11:23, where He said, "For verily I say unto you, That whosoever shall say unto this mountain, Be thou removed, and be thou cast into the sea; and shall not doubt in his heart, but shall believe that those things which he saith shall come to pass; he shall have whatsoever he saith."

Notice Jesus said this person "shall not doubt in his heart." The word "doubt" here really means *to differ*. Thus, Jesus is saying, "If your heart and mouth are saying the same thing God says and there's no *differing* between them, you've come into full agreement with God on that issue. It is a position of divine alignment, and in that position, a door for God's power to flow through you opens — a power so great you can even speak to a mountain, and it will be removed."

This is a clear picture of confession (*homologia*). Unfortunately, many believers do not understand this. They think confession only has to do with the mouth — just saying the right thing. But that is incorrect. You can say the right thing with your mouth but not fully believe it in your heart, and you will not receive what you say. To experience the supernatural power of God through confession, Jesus said there can be no differing between your mouth and your heart.

Are You Just 'Parroting' What God Said?

Rick shared a humorous story of what happened many years ago when he was staying in a pastor's home where he was ministering. At about five o'clock in the morning, he was suddenly awakened by the sound of the phone ringing in the kitchen. *Surely someone is going to get that phone*, he thought. But the phone kept ringing and ringing.

With no end to the ringing in sight, Rick began counting the rings. *That's twenty*, he said to himself. *Twenty-five....* Still, no one answered the phone. *Thirty...thirty-five.* Finally, after about forty rings he said, "Well, if nobody else is going to answer the phone, I'll get up, go upstairs, and answer it myself."

Frustrated, he put on his robe, climbed the steps, and walked down the hallway to the kitchen. With the sound of the phone ringing now intensified, he reached over to answer it. "Hello," he said now fully awake. But the phone just kept ringing!

Suddenly, he noticed a large, covered birdcage off to the side. When he pulled the cover off the cage, there was a large parrot sitting on its perch mimicking the ringing of a telephone. Clearly, the parrot was not a phone — but it sounded just like one!

In the same way, people sometimes make confessions of faith that sound like real confessions, but they are not. Although everything coming out of their mouth is right, it's not coming from their heart. They are just "parroting" what they've heard, and since there's a differing between their mouth and the heart, nothing's going to take place. Again, Jesus said in Mark 11:23 that the mouth and the heart have to be in agreement; there can be no differing between the two. When the mouth and heart get into agreement, a channel is formed through which God's power moves and supernatural things take place.

Coming Into Agreement With God Is a Prerequisite To Experiencing His Power

Friend, when God gives you a promise, a dream, or a word of instruction, your mouth and heart have to come into agreement with what God has said. And sometimes that is a process, which is what we see happening all throughout the Scriptures.

Think about **Enoch**. He received a word from God that he would never see death. The Bible says, "By faith Enoch was taken away so that he did not see death, 'and was not found, because God had taken him'..." (Hebrews 11:5 *NKJV*). In order for Enoch's faith to make way for the power of God to operate, he had to come into agreement with what God said. How long it took for him to get his mouth and heart in divine alignment, the Bible doesn't say. Nevertheless, he *did* come into full agreement with God and was taken to Heaven.

What about **Noah**? Hebrews 11:7 tells us, "By faith Noah, being warned of God of things not seen as yet, moved with fear, prepared an ark to the saving of his house; by the which he condemned the world, and became heir of the righteousness which is by faith." Can you imagine the internal tug of war between Noah's mind and heart? *What's a flood*, he must have thought. *And what's an ark?* He had never seen either one. Yet he had received a word from the Lord. How long it took him to get into agreement with God, we don't know. But at some point, his heart began to beat in sync with God's heart, and his obedience transformed him and his family into a mighty instrument that saved the world of that age!

How about **Abraham**? He and his wife Sarah were living in the lap of luxury in the city of Ur, when suddenly he came face to face with the God of Glory (*see* Acts 7:2). In that moment, God said, "...Get out of your country and from your relatives, and come to a land that I will show you" (Acts 7:3 *NKJV*). For Abraham to obey God, he had to get his entire being into agreement with Him until his heart was beating in sync with God on this issue.

When we come to the New Testament, we have the example of **Mary** the mother of Jesus. Scholars estimate she was somewhere between 12 and 14 years old when the angel Gabriel appeared to her with a word from God that she had been chosen to be the one who would conceive and give birth to the Son of God. For this unprecedented miracle to happen, Mary had to get into agreement with God. How long did it take for her to come into alignment with the promise she received? According to Scripture, not too long. Before Gabriel left, "…Mary said, Behold the handmaid of the Lord; be it unto me according to thy word. And the angel departed from her" (Luke 1:38).

Then there was Saul who became the apostle **Paul**. He was a Pharisee of the Pharisees, born of the tribe of Benjamin, and zealous for the preservation of Judaism. Before his conversion, he was going from town-to-town imprisoning and killing Christians. As he traveled the road to Damascus to continue his rampage, Jesus suddenly appeared to him in a blinding light and knocked him to the ground. "I'm sending you to the Gentiles," Jesus said, "to open their eyes to the truth and receive forgiveness" (*see* Acts 26:17,18). Paul spent the next three days sitting and praying in a house in Damascus. During that time, he began to come into alignment with the Lord's purpose for his life. A careful study of Paul's life reveals that it took him quite some time to fully come into agreement with God's assignment. But once he did, God used him to turn the Gentile world right-side-up!

Aligning Ourselves With God's Will Is Sometimes a Struggle

We are all uniquely different, and each of us requires a certain amount of time to come into agreement with God's calling on our lives. For some it takes longer than others. For example, when God first told Rick that he was to move his family to the former Soviet Union, he was completely confused and didn't know what to do. *Move my family to the Soviet Union?* he thought. *That doesn't make any sense.*

At that time, it was still the Soviet Union — the dilapidated land where communism and atheism ruled supreme. *How will I support my family?* he thought. *And what about my ministry in the United States? How can I keep it going and launch a brand-new ministry on the other side of the world? Where are we going to get the finances for all of this?*

Rick first received this mind-boggling new direction from the Holy Spirit while on a short-term mission trip to the Soviet Union. When he returned to the United States, he didn't say a word to anyone. But while Rick was quiet, the Lord kept talking. Day after day He would ask Rick, "Are you going to obey me?" Basically, what God was saying is, "Rick, are you going to get into agreement with Me? Are you going to come into divine alignment with Me and step into this new chapter of your life?"

"That is such a huge step of faith, Lord," Rick responded. *"I just don't know how I can do that."*

This tense internal conversation continued for several months, and then one day while Rick was speaking at a mission conference, the anointing of God fell heavily on the entire place. In fact, His presence was so thick in that service, Rick was moved by the Spirit to do what he hadn't been able to do since he first received the new direction from the Lord. There, in front of the entire crowd, he surrendered to God's will and publicly announced, "I am moving my family to the Soviet Union."

In that super-anointed atmosphere, Rick was overwhelmed with excitement and felt really good about the decision he had made. But by the time he returned to his room that night, he became panic-stricken. *What did I do?* he thought. *What did I say? Now that I've announced it, I have to go through with it. If I don't, people are going to think I'm disobedient or that I really don't know the voice of the Lord.*

Rick was so upset he spent the entire night on his knees, hugging the toilet and vomiting. Now, the Lord was not making him vomit. It was Rick's soul that was arguing with the will of God, and that night everything in him that was out of alignment got jerked *into* alignment. As God dealt with Rick, he came into full agreement with God so he could do what he had been asked to do.

When God reveals His plan to you, you may not immediately step into it. Like Rick, you may go through a period of adjustment, when you discover there are some things in your soul that are out of alignment. Before God's plan can really begin to operate through you, you'll have to get into full agreement with Him. You'll have to come to the place where you finally say, "Okay God, okay. I hear You loud and clear, and I surrender to Your will. I see what You want me to see and hear what You want me to hear. I choose to align myself totally to Your will. May my heart beat in sync and in agreement with Yours, in Jesus' name."

Friend, when you come into that level of agreement, you're in a position for real power to begin flowing through you. Again, that period of alignment is different for all of us. But regardless of how long it takes, do what you need to do to humble yourself before God, pour out your heart, and ask Him for the grace to cooperate with Him to jerk everything in you into alignment with Him so that His plan can come to pass in your life.

Don't 'Go to Bed' on Your Faith

There's one more thing we want to look at in Hebrews 10:23. It says, "Let us hold fast the profession of our faith without *wavering*...." Notice that word "wavering." It is the Greek word *aklines*, which is from the word *klines*, a term that describes *one who is bowed down and so tired he can barely stand*. Interestingly, the word *klines* is the same root in Greek for *a bed*. Hence, when a person is *klines*, he has a "give-up" attitude and is so exhausted *he's going to bed on his faith*.

So many believers start out strong and on fire for God. They know what He wants them to do and are passionately pursuing the dream He's placed in their heart. But after many difficulties and unexpected delays — aka *dream thieves* — they give up. Time begins to say, "It's too late. Too much time has passed. It's never going to happen." Then Satan chimes in, "What makes you think you deserve more than a mediocre life? You need to stop dreaming and come back to reality." Of course, your friends and family who really love you may also try to give you a more balanced perspective and talk you out of doing what you feel God wants you to do, and while their reasons may have merit and seem logical, they should never carry more authority than what God has spoken.

He says, "...Hold fast the profession of [your] faith without wavering..." (Hebrews 10:23). Again, "without wavering" — the Greek word *aklines* — means *don't go to bed on your faith*. In other words, be *unbending*, *unchanging*, and *unmoving* in your pursuit of the dream God has given you. Wrap your arms tightly around the promise you are confessing — embracing it with all your might and rejecting all attempts of anyone who tries to steal it from you. Friend, it's time to jerk everything in you that is out of alignment into alignment, so God's power can flow to you and through you and His plan for your life may be fulfilled.

You Have Good Reason To Keep Believing

You may be thinking, *I have believed and waited and continued doing everything I know to do to obediently walk in faith, but I still haven't seen the manifestation of what God has promised. Just give me one reason why I should keep believing.* If this is where you are, take a close look at the closing words of Hebrews 10:23. It says, "...For He is faithful that promised." God is not a man that He should lie — He's not like humans who often change their minds. What He says, He does (*see* Numbers 23:19).

The word of God is true, and if He has said He's going to do something, He will keep His word. Your job is to get into alignment with Him and hold fast to the word He's given you. There will always come a moment when you're tempted to cast away your confession because you're tired or because the dream thieves are screaming in your ears. That's when you have to grab hold of God's Word and push all the opposition out of the way. The presence of resistance is just more evidence that you're not quite in alignment yet.

If you will surrender yourself to God and cooperate with the Holy Spirit's promptings, you will come into divine alignment. Sure, it may take some time, but if you choose not to budge from where God placed you or to not let go of what He promised, the dream He gave you will come to pass. How will you know that you're in alignment with Him? When there's no differing between your mouth and your heart and the power of God begins to flow.

STUDY QUESTIONS

Study to shew thyself approved unto God, a workman that needeth not to be ashamed, rightly dividing the word of truth.
— 2 Timothy 2:15

1. When you think about the process of coming into agreement with a promise God has spoken, what person in the Bible comes to mind? What is it about their story that fascinates you and encourages you in your own walk of faith?

2. Have you ever been so exhausted that you "went to bed on your faith"? All of us get tired at times and need a reinvigoration of God's power in our lives. Take some time to meditate on these passages and

turn them into a personal prayer that invites God to empower you once again.

He [God] gives power to the faint and weary, and to him who has no might He increases strength [causing it to multiply and making it to abound].

— Isaiah 40:29 (*AMPC*)

Riches and glory come from you, you're ruler over all; You hold strength and power in the palm of your hand to build up and strengthen all.

— 1 Chronicles 29:12 (*MSG*)

[God says] "My grace is enough for you: for where there is weakness, my power is shown the more completely." Therefore, I have cheerfully made up my mind to be proud of my weaknesses, because they mean a deeper experience of the power of Christ. I can even enjoy weaknesses, suffering, privations, persecutions and difficulties for Christ's sake. For my very weakness makes me strong in him.

— 2 Corinthians 12:9,10 (*J.B. Phillips*)

PRACTICAL APPLICATION

But be ye doers of the word, and not hearers only, deceiving your own selves.
— James 1:22

1. Prior to this lesson, what was your perception of "confessing something in faith"? How has your understanding of what this means become clearer? According to Jesus, what must happen in you for true confession to take place and activate God's power in your life?

2. Rick shared how he struggled to get into full agreement with God about moving to the Soviet Union. Can you think of a situation in your life when you struggled to get into alignment with God? What was He asking you to do? Did you ever come into full agreement with Him on the issue? If so, what was it that really helped you surrender to Him?

3. The presence of resistance is actually evidence that you're not quite in alignment yet with what God is asking you to do. Get quiet before the Lord and pray, *What is out of alignment in my heart and soul, Lord? Why*

is my soul (my mind, will, and emotions) still unsettled with what You're asking me to do? Please show me that I might surrender it to You and receive Your grace to come into divine alignment. In Jesus' name.

LESSON 4

TOPIC

Do Not Give Up on Your Faith

SCRIPTURES

1. **Hebrews 10:23** — Let us hold fast the profession of our faith without wavering; (for he is faithful that promised).

2. **Hebrews 10:35** — Cast not away therefore your confidence, which hath great recompence of reward.

3. **Mark 10:50** — And he, casting away his garment, rose, and came to Jesus.

4. **Hebrews 10:36-39** — For ye have need of patience, that, after ye have done the will of God, ye might receive the promise. For yet a little while, and he that shall come will come, and will not tarry. Now the just shall live by faith: but if any man draw back, my soul shall have no pleasure in him. But we are not of them who draw back unto perdition; but of them that believe to the saving of the soul.

GREEK WORDS

1. "hold fast" — **κατέχω** (*katecho*): to embrace something tightly, and because of the preposition **κατα** (*kata*), it is the image of someone who finds the object of his dreams and then holds it down — even to the point of sitting on it — in order to dominate and take control of it; to suppress

2. "cast" — **ἀποβάλλω** (*apoballo*): to throw away; to discard; to get rid of something no longer desired, needed, or wanted

3. "confidence" — **παρρησία** (*parresia*): pictures bold, frank, forthright speech; confidence; audacity; pictures an attitude that is emboldened or extraordinarily frank; a daring to speak what one believes or thinks, possibly even in the face of retribution; boldness; assurance;

unashamed confidence; a frankness of speech that accompanies unflinching authority

4. "great" — **μέγα** (*mega*): enormous, giant, great

5. "recompense of reward" — **μισθαποδοσία** (*misthapodosia*): the word for money, salary, or a payment that is due; primarily used to denote a payment, salary, or reward given for a job performed; recompense, reimbursement, settlement, or reparation; being reimbursed for an expense a person has paid out of his own pocket

6. "need" — **χρεία** (*chreia*): a lack, deficit, shortage

7. "patience" — **ὑπομονή** (*hupomone*): to stay or to abide; to remain in one's spot; to keep a position; to resolve to maintain territory that has been gained; in a military sense, pictures soldiers who were ordered to maintain their positions even in the face of fierce combat; to defiantly stick it out, regardless of the pressure mounted against it; endurance; staying power; "hang-in-there" power; the attitude that holds out, holds on, outlasts, perseveres, and hangs in there, never giving up, refusing to surrender to obstacles, and turning down every opportunity to quit; pictures one who is under a heavy load but refuses to bend, break, or surrender because he is convinced that the territory, promise, or principle under assault rightfully belongs to him; stamina, durability

8. "receive" — **κομίζω** (*komidzo*): receive; to receive what is due; to receive what one has coming to him

9. "little while" — **Μικρὸν ὅσον ὅσον** (*mikron hoson hoson*): a very, very little while; depicts something small or tiny; where we get the word microscopic

10. "not tarry" — **οὐ χρονίσει** (*ou chronesei*): will not be late, will not be delayed, will not be chronologically out of order

11. "draw back" — **ὑποστέλλω** (*hupostello*): to shrink back; one who is withdrawing, retreating, regressing, receding, backing away, backsliding, or recoiling from something; one who reverses his direction; to move backward instead of forward; to back off and retreat from an object, principle, or task

12. "no pleasure" — **οὐκ εὐδοκεῖ** (*ouk eudokei*): emphatically will not find pleasing

13. "perdition" — **ἀπώλεια** (*apoleia*): something ruined, rotten, and decomposing; used to describe the stench of a decaying animal or a dead human body; a loathsome, putrid, vulgar, disgusting, nauseating

scent; something in the process of perishing; doomed, rotten, ruinous, or decaying

14. "but" — ἀλλὰ (*alla*): but on the contrary
15. "saving" — περιποίησις (*peripoiesis*): full acquisition; preserving; possessing; taking full ownership of
16. "soul" — ψυχή (*psuche*): mind, will, emotions; where we get the word psychology

SYNOPSIS

Hopefully it's becoming clearer that when you launch out to do what God has asked you to do, you're going to run into roadblocks and hurdles along the way. We call these *dream thieves*, and the devil uses them against you because he doesn't want you to succeed in your calling. He knows that if you carry out the assignment God has given you, people's lives will be forever changed. Many will be saved, broken lives will be restored, and your life will be blessed in extraordinary ways.

In Lesson 3, we learned that a major reason people never see their dream or vision become a reality is because they never come to a place of divine alignment. The fact is when you receive a word from the Lord — instructing you to do something different than you're used to doing — you find out rather quickly just how aligned you are with God.

Always keep in mind that while God's desire is to bless you, ultimately His plan is to transform you into the image of Jesus. As you align yourself with Him, your heart begins to beat in sync with His. The more you surrender to Him, the more you come into divine alignment with His will for your life, and the more you become like Jesus.

The emphasis of this lesson:

Once you know God has spoken to you and given you a promise, a word, or a dream, you have to "hold fast" to what He's said. When you hold tightly to and believe what He has planted in your heart, He guarantees to fully repay you for everything you've invested to bring it about. If you'll hold on in faith and keep doing what He's told you to do, you'll receive what He promised if you don't bail out.

Vital Points To Remember
From Lessons 1, 2, and 3

Looking at Hebrews 10:23, our anchor verse, it says, "Let us hold fast the profession of our faith without wavering; (for he is faithful that promised)." We've seen that the phrase "hold fast" is a translation of the Greek word *katecho*, which is a compound of the words *kata* and *echo*. The word *kata* always carries the idea of *something that's coming down so hard* that it's *dominating*, it's *conquering*, or it's *subjugating*. The second part of the word is *echo*, which means *I have, I hold, I possess*. When compounded, the new word *katecho* — translated here as "hold fast" — pictures someone who has found the dream for which he's been searching. He is so thrilled, he wraps his arms around it, holds it tightly, sits on it, and does everything he can to make sure no one takes it away from him.

Indeed, there are dream thieves in life, and they have a way of robbing us of what God has placed in our hearts if we're not watchful. The four primary dream thieves that come against all of us are:

Dream Thief #1: Time. When time passes and your dream remains unfulfilled, the clock and calendar seem to have a nagging voice that says, "It's too late. If it was going to happen, surely it would have happened by now. Just let it go."

Dream Thief #2: Satan. Along with time is the voice of the devil himself who seems to whisper in your ear, "You're just a foolish dreamer with an overactive imagination. You concocted this idea yourself and claim God spoke to you."

Dream Thief #3: Friends. Those who love and care about you want the very best for you. Out of great concern, your friends will often try to offer a more balanced perspective of the hardships you could encounter if you go in the new direction you feel God is leading you.

Dream Thief #4: Family. No one knows you like family. They've watched you for a long time. They know your weaknesses and your failures and have heard you say you were going to do certain things in the past that you never did. To help you avoid additional hurt and pain, they may try to talk you out of moving forward with your plans.

Keep in mind, that your family is your family, and (in most cases) they love you dearly. So don't argue or get offended by them. Respectfully listen to what they want to say and thank them for expressing their concern. Ultimately, if you know God has spoken to you, you have to stick with what He has said — you must "hold fast" to the confession of your faith.

'Cast Not Away Your Confidence'

It's important to note that the readers being addressed in the book of Hebrews were a group of believers who were really struggling in their faith. It appears they had been waiting and believing for God to answer their prayers for a very long time, but they had yet to see any manifestation of His promises. Thus, they were about to let go of their dream, which is why the writer said, "Cast not away therefore your confidence, which hath great recompence of reward" (Hebrews 10:35).

The word "cast" here is a translation of the Greek word *apoballo*, which is a compound of the word *apo*, meaning *away*, and the word *ballo*, meaning *to throw*. When these words are combined to form the word *apoballo*, it means *to throw away; to discard; or to get rid of something no longer desired, needed, or wanted*. This same word *apoballo* is used in Mark 10:50, when blind Bartimaeus was trying to get to Jesus. He had been sitting by the roadway wrapped in a garment of some kind. When he heard that Jesus was passing by, the Bible says, "And he, casting away his garment, rose, and came to Jesus." The phrase "casting away" is *apoballo*. Hindered by the garment wrapped around him, Bartimaeus ripped it off and threw it aside in order to get to Jesus to receive his healing.

The writer of Hebrews used this same word *apoballo* — translated as "cast not away" — to urge believers *not to throw away* or *discard their confidence*. After having waited and waited for God to answer their prayers, they had become quite weary and were tempted to rid themselves of what seemed to be a fairy-tale promise and move on with their lives. Indeed, the struggle to keep believing and trusting God when nothing seems to be happening is very real. It's possible that these believers were thinking, *What's the use to keep believing? If God was going to do something, surely He would have done it by now. Our faith is just a hindrance that is keeping us from getting where we want to be.*

To this kind of thinking, the writer of Hebrews pleaded, "Cast not away therefore your confidence…" (Hebrews 10:35). The word "confidence" is a translation of the Greek word *parresia*, and it describes *a bold, frank, forthright kind of speech*. It depicts *confidence* or *one that is audacious or emboldened.* It denotes *openness* and carries the idea of being *extraordinarily frank.* It is *daring to speak what one believes or thinks without hesitation — possibly even in the face of retribution.* Furthermore, it pictures *boldness, assurance,* and *unashamed confidence that accompanies unflinching authority.*

The use of the word *parresia* — translated here as "confidence" — tells us that the Hebrew believers being addressed were very bold and audacious in their confession of faith when they first began their walk with God. But because their answers hadn't come yet, they were tempted to throw it all away as though the manifestation was never going to come to pass.

Holding Tightly to God's Promise Has 'Great Recompence of Reward'

We are urged not to cast away our confidence — our bold, unashamed declaration of faith — because it "…hath great recompence of reward" (Hebrews 10:35). The word "great" here is *mega* in Greek and describes *something enormous, giant,* or *great.* The phrase "recompence of reward" is taken from the Greek word *misthapodosia,* which is the term for *money, salary, or a payment that is due.* It is primarily used to denote *a payment, salary, or reward given for a job well performed.* It can also describe *a recompense, reimbursement, settlement, or reparation.* It means *to be reimbursed for an expense a person has paid out of his own pocket in order to get his job done, a full and complete recompense.*

The use of this word *misthapodosia* lets us know that if we feel as though we've wasted time along the way, or we've spent a great deal of money that we didn't have to spend, but we stayed in faith, God is going to reimburse us for everything. If we will just stay in faith and hold tightly to the promise God gave us, payday is coming! So don't throw away your confidence.

Here the writer of Hebrews basically says, "If you will hang on and continue to boldly confess your faith in God, payday is coming! He is going to reimburse you for everything you've given out."

'Patience' Is Supernatural Endurance

Then in the very next verse, the writer adds, "For ye have need of patience, that, after ye have done the will of God, ye might receive the promise" (Hebrews 10:36). Although this was probably the last thing this group of believers wanted to hear, it was what they *needed* to hear. As a matter of fact, the word "need" in this verse confirms their condition. It is the Greek word *chreia*, and it denotes *a lack, deficit,* or *shortage*. These believers were notably lacking patience.

The word "patience" is the remarkable Greek word *hupomone*, and it is packed with meaning. It is a compound of the word *hupo*, meaning *under*, and the word *meno*, meaning *to stay* or *to abide*. When compounded to form the word *hupomone*, it means *to stay or to abide; to remain in one's spot*; or *to keep a position*. It indicates *a resolve to maintain territory that has been gained*. It is to be *immovable* until what is being prayed for manifests. In a military sense, it pictures soldiers who were ordered to maintain their positions even in the face of fierce combat.

Moreover, the word "patience" (*hupomone*) means *to defiantly stick it out regardless of the pressure mounted against it*. It embodies the idea of *endurance; staying power*, or *hang-in-there power*. It is *the attitude that holds out, holds on, outlasts, perseveres, and hangs in there, never giving up, refusing to surrender to obstacles, and turning down every opportunity to quit*. This word "patience" is a picture of one who is under a heavy load but refuses to bend, break, or surrender because he is convinced that the territory, promise, or principle under assault rightfully belongs to him. This person is thoroughly committed to maintaining his position and staying in his spot as long as it's necessary for him to achieve victory. The word *hupomone* can also describe *stamina* or *durability*. A better translation of this word *hupomone* would be "endurance."

You Need Patience
To Receive God's Promises

Interestingly, this word "patience" (*hupomone*) was called the queen of virtues by the Early Church because they understood it was not a question of *if* they would win — it was a question of *when* they would win. They were holding out, holding on, and defiantly sticking to the word God had given them. Regardless of the cost, they believed that eventually all the dream thieves would be defeated, and they would receive their victory.

Friend, *hupomone* — patience — is powerful, and you need it if you're going to receive the promises of God. In fact, this verse says, "For ye have need of patience, that, after ye have done the will of God..." (Hebrews 10:36). What is the will of God? It is doing what He has told you to do, believing what He has told you to believe.

The writer states, "…After ye have done the will of God, ye might receive the promise" (Hebrews 10:36). The word "receive" is also important. In Greek, it is the word *komidzo*, which literally means *to receive what is due* or *to receive what one has coming to him*. The inclusion of this word in this passage is the equivalent of saying, "Whatever promise of God you have been declaring by faith — whatever you have been boldly speaking and believing God for — is coming to you. It is your *recompense* or *reward* that is on its way to you — as long as you don't give up."

For instance, if the dream you're holding on to is healing, healing is coming to you. If the dream you're holding on to is a new ministry, you have a new ministry coming to you. What are you believing for? Financial provision, favor, vindication of a suffered wrong, restoration of your marriage? Whatever God has promised you — whatever dream He's dropped in your heart — if you'll hold on in faith and keep doing what He's told you to do, you will receive it if you don't give up.

The Answer You've Been Waiting for Is on the Way

In Hebrews 10:37, the Bible goes on to say, "For yet a little while, and he that shall come will come, and will not tarry." In Greek, the phrase "little while" is *mikron hoson*, which means *a very, very little while* and depicts *something small* or *tiny*. The word *mikron* is where we get the word *microscopic*. Here the Holy Spirit is encouraging us by letting us know that in a *microscopic* amount of time, the answer we have been waiting for will come, and it will *not tarry*.

The words "not tarry" is a translation of the Greek phrase *ou chronesei*, which means *will not be late, will not be delayed, will not be chronologically out of order*. This tells us that God has a definite timetable, and what He has planned is going to show up right on time!

What Happens if You 'Draw Back' From God?

When we come to Hebrews 10:38, the writer makes this declaration: "Now the just shall live by faith: but if any man draw back, my soul shall have no pleasure in him." Notice the phrase "draw back." It is the Greek word *hupostello*, which means *to shrink back*. It pictures *one who is withdrawing, retreating, regressing, receding, backing away, backsliding, or recoiling from something*. It denotes *a reversal of direction — a move backward instead of forward* or *to back off and retreat from an object, principle, or task.* A person who "draws back" from what God has told him to do or to believe, God will "have no pleasure in," which means He *emphatically will not find pleasing.*

Immediately, the writer of Hebrews follows up in the next verse saying, "But we are not of them who draw back unto perdition; but of them that believe to the saving of the soul" (Hebrews 10:39). Again, we see the phrase "draw back" — the Greek word *hupostello.* In this case, he is saying, "We are *not* the kind of people that *shrink back, withdraw,* or *retreat* from our position of faith." Specifically, he said, "But we are not of them who draw back unto perdition..." (Hebrews 10:39).

The Greek word for "perdition" is *apoleia,* and it pictures *something ruined, rotten, and decomposing.* It was used to describe *the stench of a decaying animal or a dead human body.* It denoted *the smell of something loathsome, putrid, vulgar, disgusting, or nauseating; something in the process of perishing; something doomed, rotten, ruinous, or decaying.* This word *apoleia* — translated here as "perdition" — gives us a vivid picture of what happens to people who retreat from their position of faith. When they back off from or throw away what they were believing, their lives begin to emit a terrible spiritual stench and acquire a nauseating attitude of cynicism and bitterness about life as well as those who are walking in faith. If you've ever been there, you know how awful this condition can be.

'But we are not of them who draw back unto perdition....'
(Hebrews 10:39)

The opening word "but" means *on the contrary.* Rather than move in reverse or retreat, we are "...of them that believe to the saving of the soul" (Hebrews 10:39). That word, *believe,* is a form of the Greek word *pistis,* which is the same word for *faith.* Faith is a force that is moving forward and is never in retreat. Essentially, faith is like a bullet that's been shot out of a gun. Once it's been launched from the gun, it can't go backward. It must move forward. Likewise, when you release your faith, it propels you into a forward motion. If you're moving in retreat, you're not in faith.

What does the forward movement of faith produce? The Bible says, "...the saving of the soul" (Hebrews 10:39). This part of the verse reveals where our problem is — in the *soul.* The Greek word for "soul" is *psuche,* and it's where we get the word *psychology.* It specifically describes *the mind, will,* and *emotions.* Our mind is what listens to the lies of the dream thieves. When the voices of time, Satan, friends, and family begin speaking, our thinking, our feelings, and our ability to make decisions get involved and often give way to things like fear, anxiety, and confusion.

But if we will stay in faith and hold tightly to what God has spoken, our soul will be protected from the effects of the dream thieves and God will bring us into the reality of what we're believing for. So don't pull back or throw away your confidence! If you stay in faith, a great recompense of reward is on its way to you!

STUDY QUESTIONS

Study to shew thyself approved unto God, a workman that needeth not to be ashamed, rightly dividing the word of truth.
— 2 Timothy 2:15

1. When you first began your walk with God, were you bold and audacious in your confession of faith? But because answers to your prayers still haven't come, are you now being tempted to throw it all away as though the manifestation was never going to come to pass?

2. What promise does God make to you in Galatians 6:9 regarding persevering and holding on to what He has spoken to you? How are Peter's words in First Peter 5:6-10 similar to this promise?

PRACTICAL APPLICATION

But be ye doers of the word, and not hearers only, deceiving your own selves.
— James 1:22

1. Take some time to carefully reflect on the word "patience" — the Greek word *hupomone*. What new insights is the Holy Spirit showing you about this *queen of all virtues*? In what areas of your life do you see this supernatural *endurance* operating at some level? Where do you lack patience and need the Holy Spirit to develop it in you?

2. The struggle to keep believing and trusting God when nothing seems to be happening is very real. Be honest: Have you let go of or discarded a promise God has given you? If so, what is it and why have you "cast it away"?

3. The Bible says that people who "draw back" or retreat from their position of faith suffer "perdition." In your own words, describe what

"perdition" means. Have you ever experienced this condition? Are you experiencing it now?

TOPIC

The Behavior of Real Faith

SCRIPTURES

1. **Hebrews 10:38,39** — Now the just shall live by faith: but if any man draw back, my soul shall have no pleasure in him. But we are not of them who draw back unto perdition; but of them that believe to the saving of the soul.

2. **Hebrews 11:1-3** — Now faith is the substance of things hoped for, the evidence of things not seen. For by it the elders obtained a good report. Through faith we understand that the worlds were framed by the word of God, so that things which are seen were not made of things which do appear.

GREEK WORDS

1. "draw back" — ὑποστέλλω (*hupostello*): to shrink back; one who is withdrawing, retreating, regressing, receding, backing away, backsliding, or recoiling from something; one who reverses his direction; to move backward instead of forward; to back off and retreat from an object, principle, or task

2. "no pleasure" — οὐκ εὐδοκεῖ (*ouk eudokei*): emphatically will not find pleasing

3. "perdition" — ἀπώλεια (*apoleia*): something ruined, rotten, and decomposing; used to describe the stench of a decaying animal or a dead human body; a loathsome, putrid, vulgar, disgusting, nauseating scent; something in the process of perishing; doomed, rotten, ruinous, or decaying

4. "soul" — ψυχή (*psuche*): mind, will, emotions; where we get the word psychology

5. "now" — δὲ (*de*): but; on the other hand

6. "faith" — πίστις (*pistis*): its root means to persuade, to trust, to believe; a persuasion from God that imparts an impulse or "divine spark" to believe; in secular antiquity referred to a guarantee or warranty of something that was sure; a force that is propelled forward toward a goal

7. "substance" — ὑπόστασις (*hupostasis*): a compound of ὑπό (*hupo*) and ἵστημι (*histimi*); the preposition ὑπό (*hupo*) means by, and the word ἵστημι (*histimi*) means to stand; literally, to stand by something; the attitude and actions of one who has determined to stand by something promised and refuses to budge from it; a fixed decision that one will be unmoving and he will stay or stand by a person, principle, promise, or territory

8. "hoped for" — ἐλπίζω (*elpidzo*): to actively hope for the fulfillment of something expected; the form used in this verse is continuous, "being hoped for," stressing that the manifestation has not come yet

9. "elders" — πρεσβύτεροι (*presbuteroi*): elders; the respected ones; in this case, heroes of faith

10. "we understand" — νοοῦμεν (*nooumen*): plural form of νοέω (*noeo*); to think or to understand; indicates intelligent activity; we think, we conclude, we rationalize, we understand

11. "worlds" — αἰῶνας (*aionas*): from αἰών (*aion*), an age or era; a specific time, age, or era within the past history of mankind; different periods of time

12. "framed" — καταρτίζω (*katartidzo*): to change, to mend, to adjust, or to alter the form or shape of an already existing thing; here, re-creating, reshaping, remolding, and altering something already in existence; not so much the act of creation, but the act of transformation

13. "the word of God" — ῥήματι Θεοῦ (*rhemati Theou*): in context, by a word from God

SYNOPSIS

In each of our previous lessons, we've been studying Hebrews 10:23, which in the *King James Version* says, "Let us hold fast the profession of our faith...." What you may not know is that in the original Greek text, the word "our" does not appear. The verse simply says, "Let us hold fast the profession of faith...." This indicates that "the profession of faith" is any word that God has spoken to us, whether it's a direct quote from the Scripture or a very specific promise He's spoken to each of us regarding our lives. Whatever the case, we are to hold tightly to it with all our might and come into divine alignment in our hearts with what He has spoken.

Essentially, that is the behavior of faith. And that is what is described again in Hebrews 11:1, which declares, "Now faith is the substance of things hoped for, the evidence of things not seen." Although many say that this verse defines faith, the original Greek reveals that it is not a *definition* of faith but rather a description of the *behavior* of faith. In order to avoid becoming a spiritual statistic of the dream thieves, it is imperative that you understand the meaning of this passage.

The emphasis of this lesson:

Faith behaves like a bulldog that's found the bone of its wildest dreams. It will not quit or relent under pressure. Faith resolves to believe God's Word at any cost. It's not going to move until it sees the manifestation of what He has promised. The heroes of the Old Testament operated in this kind of faith, transforming their generation and the world around them.

A Review of Hebrews 10:38,39

To help us have a better understanding of the opening verses of Hebrews 11, let's briefly review the last two verses of chapter 10. Looking at Hebrews 10:38, the writer declares: "Now the just shall live by faith: but if any man draw back, my soul shall have no pleasure in him." The word "faith" is the Greek word *pistis*, which always describes *a force that is forward moving*. It's like a bullet that has been shot from a pistol — once it leaves the barrel, it always moves forward, never in reverse. This is one sure way you can know if you are *in faith* or *out of faith*: if you're in retreat, you are *not* in faith. You are "drawing back."

Again, Hebrews 10:38 says, "…But if any man *draw back*, my soul shall have no pleasure in him." The words "draw back" are a translation of the Greek word *hupostello*, which means *to shrink back*. It pictures *one who is withdrawing, retreating, regressing, receding, backing away, backsliding, or recoiling from something*. This is *a person who is moving backward instead of forward — backing off and retreating from an object, principle, or task*. When we "draw back" from what God has told us to do or to believe, God "has no pleasure in him," which means He *emphatically will not find us pleasing*.

In direct contrast, the writer of Hebrews follows up and says, "But we are not of them who draw back unto perdition..." (Hebrews 10:39). The original Greek text here says, "*On the contrary,* we are not of them who draw back unto perdition...." In other words, "We are *not* the kind of people that *shrink back, withdraw,* or *retreat* from our position of faith." Specifically, he said, "But we are not of them who draw back unto perdition..." (Hebrews 10:39).

We saw that the Greek word for "perdition" is *apoleia,* and it pictures *something ruined, rotten, and decomposing.* It is the very word used to describe *the stench of a decaying animal or a dead human body.* It depicts *a loathsome, putrid, vulgar, disgusting,* or *nauseating smell; something in the process of perishing* or *something doomed, rotten, ruinous,* or *decaying.* In context, this word *apoleia* — translated here as "perdition" — indicates that when we begin to back away from or stop believing God's word to us, our life begins to emit a terrible spiritual stench! If you've ever been around someone who has retreated from their position of faith, they are difficult to be around. Their attitude of cynicism, negativity, and bitterness about life is nauseating.

The Bible says, "But we are not of them who draw back unto perdition..." (Hebrews 10:39). Again, the word "but" means *on the contrary.* Rather than move in reverse or retreat, we are "...of them that believe to the saving of the soul" (Hebrews 10:39). That word "soul" is the Greek word *psuche,* which is where we get the word *psychology.* It describes *the mind, will,* and *emotions.* It is our mind that comes under attack by the dream thieves. Time says, "It's too late. It's never going to happen now. You might as well give up and move on." Likewise, Satan screams, "You're just a crazy dreamer! God didn't speak to you. You're living in a fantasy world." Moreover, your friends and family members will likely offer you a series of "what-if" scenarios to paint a more realistic picture of what to expect if you step out to do what you believe God has asked you to do. If you will stay in faith, holding tightly to what God has spoken to you, your soul will be protected from the effects of the dream thieves, and in time, God will bring about what you're believing for.

The Behavior of Real Faith

Hebrews 11:1 continues talking about the subject of faith saying, "Now faith is the substance of things hoped for, the evidence of things not seen." For many believers, this verse has been rather abstract and difficult to understand. But a careful reading of this passage in the Greek New Testament reveals this verse in a whole new light.

For instance, in the original Greek, the word "now" doesn't appear. It starts out with the Greek word *de*, which is a comparative word meaning *but* or *on the other hand*. Hence, the opening of the verse would better be translated as, "*But* faith is…." It's as if the writer raises his voice and says, "Now I'm going to tell you what faith is really like. Faith is never in retreat. On the other hand, faith is the substance of things hoped for, the evidence of things not seen."

Remember, the writer of Hebrews just wrapped up Chapter 10 encouraging his readers to hold tightly to their confession of faith and not draw back into spiritual ruin and decay. In chapter 11, he shifts his focus to talk about individuals who held on to their faith and effectively changed history as a result.

"So what *is* faith?" you ask. Good question! The Bible says, "Now faith is the substance of things hoped for…" (Hebrews 11:1). The word "substance" has certainly stumped many a person, but in Greek its meaning is quite clear. It is the word *hupostasis*, which is a compound of the words *hupo* and *histimi*. The word *hupo* means *to be by something*, and the word *histimi* means *to stand*. When these two words are compounded to form *hupostasis*, it literally means *to stand by something*. It is *the attitude and actions of one who has determined to stand by something promised and who refuses to budge from it*. It denotes *a fixed decision that one will be unmoving, and he will stay or stand by a person, principle, promise, or territory*. Thus, faith *stands by things hoped for* (the promises of God).

In many ways, faith behaves like a bulldog that has found the bone of its wildest dreams. Driven by insatiable desire, that dog tenaciously wraps its jaws around that bone as if its life depended on it. No matter how hard you tug or try to pull that bone away, that dog has decided it's going to hang on to its bone and never let it go. That is the idea being communicated through the word "substance." We could call it "bull-dog" faith.

This is a faith that will not bend under pressure and has resolved to believe at any cost. Rain or shine, sink or swim, it's not going to move until it sees the manifestation of what God has promised. With this in mind, we could translate Hebrews 11:1 as, "Now faith is tirelessly and determinedly standing by and never letting go of things hoped for…."

Faith latches hold of the Word of God and/or a promise from Him and doesn't let go until it becomes a reality. For example, if you're sick and you're believing for healing, faith will latch hold of God's healing promises. Regardless of the doctor's report, you wrap your jaws of faith around Scripture and won't let loose of that promise that has been made to you. Similarly, if God has made you a promise about your finances, but they seem to be under assault, or about your marriage that seems to be falling apart, faith holds on tightly and tirelessly stands by God's promises and never lets go. Bull-dog faith never bends, never brakes, never retires, and never gives up. It stands by what has been promised.

The Bible says we are to stand by and hold tightly to "...things hoped for..." (Hebrews 11:1). The phrase "hoped for" is a translation of the Greek word *elpidzo*, which means *to actively hope for the fulfillment of something expected*. Although it has not happened yet, there is an active expectation that what you are believing for will take place. The form of the word *elpidzo* here is *continuous*. Hence, it is something being hoped for, stressing that the manifestation has not come yet. Again, this is more of a description of how faith behaves rather than a definition of what faith is.

The Old Testament Heroes Operated in Faith and Changed the World

When we come to Hebrews 11:2, we are given a specific example of how faith acts. It says, "For by it [faith] the elders obtained a good report." How did the elders obtain a good report? They did it by bull-dog faith that never bends, never breaks, never quits, and never lets go but tirelessly stands by the promise that has been made. The word "elders" here is the Greek word *presbuteroi*, which means *the respected ones*, and in this case refers to *the heroes of faith in Old Testament times*.

The Bible goes on to say, "Through faith we understand that the worlds were framed by the word of God... (Hebrews 11:3)." When many people first read this verse, they think it refers to the days of creation that are talked about in Genesis, but when we read it in the original Greek text, we see that it is actually referring to the unbendable, unbreakable, never-give-up faith of the elders or Old Testament heroes who obtained a good report.

Basically, Hebrews 11:3 says, "Through 'faith' — (*pistis*) *the unflinching, immovable, never-give-up trust and belief in what God has said* — we understand that the worlds were framed by the word of God...." The phrase "we understand" is a translation of the Greek word *nooumen*, which is the plural form of the word *noeo*, meaning *to think* or *to understand*. This word indicates *intelligent activity* and could be translated as *we think, we conclude, we rationalize*, or *we understand*. What did these believers understand, rationalize, and conclude when they studied the heroes of old? That the worlds were framed by the word of God.

Here is where many people get confused. The word "worlds" here is not the Greek word *geis*, which describes the *planet*, or the Greek word *kosmos*, which describes the *universe*. Instead, the word "worlds" is the Greek word *aionas*, which is from the word *aion*, and it describes *an age or era*. It is *a specific time, age,* or *era within the past history of mankind* or *different periods of time*. The word *aionas* would never be used to describe creation. In light of this fact, this portion of Hebrews 11:3 could be translated: "Through faith we've looked at, studied, rationalized, and concluded that the different ages or eras within the past history of mankind were framed by the word of God."

This brings us to the word "framed," the Greek word *katartidzo*, which means *to change, to mend, to adjust,* or *to alter the form or shape of an already existing thing*. It carries the idea of *re-creating, reshaping, remolding, and altering something already in existence*. Hence, it is not so much the act of creation, but the act of *transformation*. It is also important to note that the phrase "the word of God" in Greek would better be translated as *by a word from God*.

Taking the Greek meaning of all these key words, the first part of Hebrews 11:3 would better be translated:

> "Through faith — through the unbendable, unbreakable, never-give-up kind of faith that stands by what it's hoping for in God's Word — we understand and conclude that the different ages and different generations (decades, centuries, and millennia) in the past history of mankind have been framed — altered, modified, and radically changed — by individuals who received a word from God...."

Extraordinary Things Happen
When You Believe With Bulldog Faith

The verse goes on to say, "...So that things which are seen were not made of things which do appear" (Hebrews 11:3). Essentially, this is telling us that by the time these elders or heroes of the Old Testament were finished believing God to fulfill His promises, they left their generation (age or era) and the world differently than how they entered it. This fits perfectly with the remainder of Hebrews 11, which details many of the heroes of the faith who aligned themselves with the word they received from God and tenaciously stood by it, regardless of how long it took to see it become a reality.

Think about ordinary people like Noah and Abraham who each received a word from God. Because they faithfully stood by that word, they adjusted, amended, and changed their generations and left the world better than they found it.

In the same way, when you receive a word from God and believe it with bulldog faith, extraordinary things are going to happen! That is why Satan is fighting so hard to get you to cast away your confidence and let go of the promise God has given you. He knows that if you will tenaciously stand by the word God has spoken, you will change your generation. You will transform your family, your business, your church, and the world in which you live.

Keep in mind that "...Without faith it is impossible to please him [God]..." (Hebrews 11:6). As we will see clearly in the lessons ahead, this verse literally means, *outside of the place of faith where God has called you, you cannot please Him.* So friend, it's time to latch hold of what God has promised with all your might. As you stay in a place of faith, you will please God and receive His promise.

STUDY QUESTIONS

Study to shew thyself approved unto God, a workman that needeth not to be ashamed, rightly dividing the word of truth.
— 2 Timothy 2:15

1. Prior to this lesson, what was your understanding of Hebrews 11:1? How do you now see this verse differently — especially in light of the Greek meaning of the words "substance" and "hoped for"?

2. Hebrews 11:3 says, "Through faith we understand that the worlds were framed by the word of God...." Did you think this verse was talking about the creation account in Genesis? Given the original Greek meaning of the word "elders" in Hebrews 11:2 and the meaning of the words "worlds," "framed," and "the word of God" in verse 3, what is actually being said here? Why is this important to the development of your faith?

3. What specific promise — or promises — has God given you from His Word or spoken to you by His Spirit that you have seen Him bring to pass in your life?

PRACTICAL APPLICATION

**But be ye doers of the word, and not hearers only,
deceiving your own selves.
—James 1:22**

1. "The profession of faith" is any word that God has spoken to you, whether it's a direct quote from the Scriptures, or a very specific promise He's given you. That said, what is YOUR profession of faith right now — what word from God are you holding on to and believing Him to bring about in your life?

2. One sure way you can know if you are *in faith* or *out of faith* is that if you're in retreat — if you are "drawing back" — you are *not* in faith. Given this test, would you say you are living *in faith* or *out of faith*? What evidence in your life supports your answer? Is there an area of your life that seems to "stink"? If so, what is it?

TOPIC

Sustaining the Fire in Your Heart

SCRIPTURES

1. **Jeremiah 1:5** — Before I formed thee in the belly I knew thee; and before thou camest forth out of the womb I sanctified thee, and I ordained thee a prophet unto the nations.

2. **Galatians 1:15,16** — ...God, who separated me from my mother's womb, and called me by his grace, to reveal his Son in me, that I might preach him among the heathen....

3. **Proverbs 29:18** — Where there is no vision, the people perish....

4. **1 Corinthians 9:24-26** — Know ye not that they which run in a race run all, but one receiveth the prize? So run, that ye may obtain. And every man that striveth for the mastery is temperate in all things. Now they do it to obtain a corruptible crown; but we an incorruptible. I therefore so run, not as uncertainly; so fight I, not as one that beateth the air.

5. **Hebrews 6:12** — That ye be not slothful, but followers of them who through faith and patience inherit the promises.

6. **Hebrews 10:23** — Let us hold fast the profession of our faith without wavering; (for he is faithful that promised).

GREEK WORDS

1. "obtain" — **καταλαμβάνω** (*katalambano*): to seize; to grab hold of; to pull down; to tackle; to conquer; to master; to hold under one's power

2. "slothful" — **νωθρός** (*nothros*): slow and sluggish; something that has lost its speed or momentum; conveying the idea of something that has lost the drive, thrust, impetus, pace, and speed it once possessed; the idea of one whose zeal has now dissipated; denotes a person who has become disinterested and whose zeal has been replaced with a middle-of-the-road, take-it-or-leave-it mentality; it carries the idea of one who has a lethargic, lackadaisical, apathetic, indifferent, lukewarm attitude toward life; a non-achiever or non-achieving attitude

SYNOPSIS

In our previous lessons, we looked closely at Ephesians 1:4, which declares that "...[God] hath chosen us in him, before the foundation of the world...." We've seen that the word "chosen" is a translation of the Greek word *eklegomai* — a compound of the word *ek*, meaning *out*, and a form of the word *lego*, meaning *I say*. When these words are combined, the new word *eklegomai* — translated here as "chosen" — means that God saw us and said, "Hey, you there! Out!" And He summoned and selected us to be His very own "before the foundation of the world."

The word "before" is the Greek word *pro*, which here indicates *long in advance of* the foundation of the world. The Greek word for "foundation" is *katabole*, which is a compound of the words *kata* and *ballo*. Kata describes *something going downward*, and the word *ballo* means *to throw* or *to hurl*. Basically, what God is saying through the use of all these words is that long before God's word ever hurled the first layers of the universe into their place, He already saw us and called us out to be His own. And according to Ephesians 2:10, when He summoned us forth, He also established specific works in which we are to walk.

Thus, we are not an afterthought or an accident. Rather, God has special things designed for each of us to do — dreams or callings, which He has placed in our hearts that we are to fulfill during our lifetime. When the dream thieves of life try to stop us from fulfilling our destiny, we must choose to "hold fast our profession of faith" (Hebrews 10:23).

The emphasis of this lesson:

Our life's goal should be to run after and seize what God has called us to do until we have tackled it and mastered it. To avoid becoming a victim of the dream thief of neutrality, we must strive to sustain the fire of God in our hearts and pursue our purpose with everything we've got. This is achieved by regularly reading the Word, praying in tongues, and surrounding ourselves with people of like faith.

God Defined Your Purpose *Before* You Were Born

The main goal of every believer should be to find God's plan for their lives and then pursue it with all their might and strength. Doing God's will and fulfilling the purpose for which we were born must be our greatest desire and our highest aspiration in life.

Keep in mind, the Bible says God chose you before the foundation of the world and that He was intimately involved in your development in your mother's womb. David makes this very clear in Psalm 139:13-16, and it is echoed by other writers — including both Jeremiah and the apostle Paul. Under the inspiration of the Holy Spirit, they declared:

> **Then the word of the Lord came unto me [Jeremiah], saying, before I formed thee in the belly I knew thee; and before thou camest forth out of the womb I sanctified thee, and I ordained thee a prophet unto the nations.**
>
> **—Jeremiah 1:4,5**

> **But when it pleased God, who separated me from my mother's womb, and called me by his grace, to reveal his Son in me, that I might preach him among the heathen; immediately I conferred not with flesh and blood.**
>
> **— Galatians 1:15,16**

Just as God chose these men, ordained them, and anointed them for His purposes before they were ever formed in their mother's wombs, He did the same for you. You're not an afterthought or an accident. The question is: Do you know God's purpose for your life, and if you do, are you pursuing its fulfillment with all your might and strength?

We Are To 'Run' After and 'Obtain' the Vision God Gave Us

There's something about knowing God's plan and purpose for our life that gives us direction and provides a bull's-eye to aim at for the decisions we need to make. Without this sense of direction, people have a tendency to flounder and wander aimlessly through life. This is precisely why Proverbs 29:18 tells us, "Where there is no vision, the people perish...." This same verse in the *New International Version* says, "Where there is no revelation, people cast off restraint...."

How are the words "vision" and "revelation" connected? When you receive a vision for your life, you have a revelation of what you have been birthed on the earth to do. "Where there is no revelation, people cast off restraint..." (Proverbs 29:18 *NIV*). The phrase "cast off restraint" is a picture of people with no goal, no purpose, no sense of direction, no motivation, and no bull's-eye at which to aim their lives. Without a sense of destiny to go after, they wander aimlessly from one thing to another.

The apostle Paul was aware of this truth, which is what motivated him to write First Corinthians 9:24-26:

> **Know ye not that they which run in a race run all, but one receiveth the prize? So run, that ye may obtain. And every man that striveth for the mastery is temperate in all things. Now they do it to obtain a corruptible crown; but we an incorruptible. I therefore so run, not as uncertainly; so fight I, not as one that beateth the air.**

Notice Paul instructed us to "…run, that ye may obtain." First, the word "run" is a translation of the Greek word *trechos*, which means *to run*. It is the picture of a person who has jumped into the race and is pressing ahead with all his might to reach his goal. He is moving at such a rapid pace that both feet never hit the ground at the same time. Paul says we are to be running this fast so that we may *obtain* the prize.

The word "obtain" here is the Greek word *katalambano*, a compound of the words *kata* and *lambano*. The word *kata* carries the idea of *something that's dominating, conquering, or subjugating*, and the word *lambano* means *I receive*. When these words are compounded to form *katalambano*, it literally means *to seize, to grab hold of, to pull down, to tackle, to conquer, to master*, or *to hold under one's power*. The use of this word tells us that our goal should be to seize whatever it is that God has called us to do until we have tackled it and mastered it.

Pursue Your Purpose With Everything You've Got

Our understanding of the assignment and our willingness to do exactly what God has called us to do will affect the amount of time it takes to "obtain" the goal. This is why it is so important for us to get into divine alignment with God so that the process moves more swiftly. To be clear — our goal is not to try to do just a little and then quit. God wants us to continue until we have accomplished what it is that He wants us to do.

So what does God want *you* to do? Go to school? Get married? Have children? Start a business? Go into the ministry? Whatever the case may be, you can't just *try* it to achieve it; you've got to run with such earnestness that you may obtain the prize. That means you've got to be like a runner who never looks back and always keeps his eyes on the finish line. Rather than approach this spiritual race lazily and half-heartedly, you've got to utilize everything that's in you and determine that you will do what God has called you to do.

Indeed, Paul kept one thing very preeminent in his thinking: "I press toward the mark for the prize of the high calling of God in Christ Jesus" (Philippians 3:14). This "high calling of God" was the purpose for which he had been brought into the world. Thus, Paul lived with a sense of destiny. The fact is that dreams come in all sizes. Some people are believing God to touch the world, while others are trusting Him for the grace to touch their city or their family. The size of the dream doesn't matter as long as you know God has given it. All assignments have one goal in common: each is strategic for changing people's lives. Once we know what we're to do, we have to run with all of our might and do whatever we have to do to obtain it.

For example, Acts 18:3 tells us when Paul first arrived in Corinth, he worked as a tentmaker in order to make ends meet. Furthermore, Paul said when he was with the Jews, he became like a Jew to reach the Jews with the message of Jesus (see 1 Corinthians 9:20). Likewise, when he was with those who were "without the law," he became like one without the law that he might win them to Christ (see 1 Corinthians 9:21). Basically, he was willing to become "…all things to all men, that [he] might by all means save some" (1 Corinthians 9:22). This tells us Paul's number one goal in life was not his own creature comfort but doing whatever he had to do to achieve the prize of his calling. This is the same way we are to live and what it means to "…run that you may obtain" (1 Corinthians 9:24).

Neutrality Is Another Major Dream Thief

In addition to the four dream thieves we have examined, there are several others that can also stop us in our tracks. *Neutrality* is another such dream thief, and it is one of the most paralyzing enemies you'll ever face. The Bible addresses this troublemaker in Hebrews 6:12, where it says, "That ye be not slothful, but followers of them who through faith and patience inherit the promises."

At first glance, you might mistake the word "slothful" to mean lazy, but that is not the case. Here, "slothful" is the Greek word *nothros*, which means *to be slow and sluggish*. It describes *something that has lost its speed or momentum* and conveys the idea of *something that has lost the drive, thrust, impetus, pace, and speed it once possessed.* It indicates *one whose zeal has now dissipated* and denotes *a person who has become disinterested and whose zeal has been replaced with a middle-of-the-road, take-it-or-leave-it mentality.* Moreover, the word *nothros* carries the idea of *one who has a lethargic, lackadaisical, apathetic, indifferent, or lukewarm attitude toward life*; hence, *a non-achiever or non-achieving attitude.*

When do people become slothful? It's usually after they've waited and waited and waited for their dream to come to pass, and still nothing has happened. As the dream thieves begin to assault this person's mind, he or she becomes tired, and slothfulness begins to set in. First, the dream thief of time says, "Just give up. You've waited long enough. If it was going to happen, it would have happened by now. Let it go."

Of course, *Satan* also chimes in and begins to whisper things like, *"You're crazy! You've dreamed all this up; you don't really have a word from God. You're living in a fantasy world."* Then there's dream thief number three — the voice of your *friends.* Primarily out of genuine concern, they try to offer a more balanced and realistic view of what you're about to do. Coupled with their voice is the voice of your *family,* who really love you and desperately want to keep you from another painful mistake.

If you get beyond all these, you often run into the dream thief of *neutrality.* Exhaustion sets in and you become indifferent, lethargic, and lose your momentum. Consequently, you develop a take-it-or-leave-it mentality that is lukewarm toward life and the things of God — an attitude Jesus really doesn't like.

The Church of Laodicea Was Plagued by Neutrality

No place is this clearer than in the book of Revelation where Jesus addressed the Church of Laodicea. He said, "I know thy works, that thou art neither cold nor hot: I would thou wert cold or hot. So then because thou art lukewarm, and neither cold nor hot, I will spue thee out of my mouth" (Revelation 3:15,16).

To fully grasp what Jesus is saying here about being lukewarm, you need to understand that Laodicea was a city without a natural source of water. To overcome this problem, it constructed a pipeline to bring in cold water from the city of Colossae to the south, and a pipeline to bring in hot water from the natural springs in the city of Hierapolis to the north. It was an engineering system of pipes unlike any other, and the citizens were excited about it.

Unfortunately, by the time the cold water that came from Colossae and the hot water that came from Hierapolis arrived in Laodicea, both had become lukewarm due to the long distance it had to travel through all the pipes. Even worse, by the time the water reached Laodicea, minerals from the pipes themselves had leached out and dissolved in the moving water, making it so distasteful that the people would spit it out.

So, when Jesus said, "...Because thou art lukewarm, and neither cold nor hot, I will spue thee out of my mouth" (Revelation 3:16), the people knew exactly what He meant. These believers were no longer on fire (hot) for God and no longer refreshing like the cold mountain waters from Colossae. They had become *neutral*, and like the mineral-laden, lukewarm water that Laodicea was known for, these lukewarm Christians made Jesus sick to His stomach — so sick He said He would vomit them out of His mouth. The fact that they were lukewarm didn't mean they had lost their salvation. It means they had lost their fiery passion and devotion to Jesus and were no longer convicted and moved by what once moved them.

Strive To Sustain the Fire of God In Your Heart

Friend, this is a sobering warning to us as believers living in the last of the last days, a time that many view as the Laodicean church age. Therefore, we must strive to sustain the fire of God in our hearts. How, you ask? By regularly reading the Word, praying in tongues, surrounding ourselves with people of like faith, and doing whatever we need to do to maintain our zeal and our passion for Jesus and the dream He's placed in our hearts.

It's time that we do what Paul urged Timothy to do — to stir up the gift of God that is in us (*see* 2 Timothy 1:6). Likewise, "Let us hold fast the profession of our faith without wavering; (for he is faithful that promised)" (Hebrews 10:23). And let us take to heart the words of Hebrews 6:12, which says, "...Be not slothful [neutral], but followers of them who through faith and patience inherit the promises."

In Lesson 7, we will focus our attention on how faith and patience work together to produce the promises of God in our lives.

STUDY QUESTIONS

**Study to shew thyself approved unto God, a workman that
needeth not to be ashamed, rightly dividing the word of truth.**
— 2 Timothy 2:15

Paul was willing to become "...all things to all men, that [he] might by
all means save some" (1 Corinthians 9:22). His number one goal in life
was not his own creature comfort, but to do whatever he had to do to
achieve the prize of his calling. What does the Bible say about Moses and
Jesus that illustrates this same determination? *See* Hebrews 11:24-26 and
Philippians 2:3-8.

Neutrality is a lethargic, lackadaisical, or apathetic attitude toward life that
lulls us into a sluggish state when it comes to the things of God. This can
have dire consequences, both for us and others. The story of Eli — the
priest who trained Samuel as he was growing up — is a prime example of
this. How did his apathetic response to his sons affect him and ultimately
his entire lineage? What does this tell you about the importance of
holding on to your momentum? (*See* 1 Samuel 2-4.)

PRACTICAL APPLICATION

But be ye doers of the word, and not hearers only,
deceiving your own selves.
— James 1:22

1. Are you exhausted? Does work feel like a Godforsaken wilderness?
   Are you dealing with health or financial problems that seem like
   they'll never go away? In what specific areas of life have you lost hope
   and feel as though your dreams are irrevocably lost?

2. Take some time to write out where you feel disappointed by unfulfilled hopes. Pray through them. If you feel numb or angry, tell God
   about it. If years' worth of uncried tears well up, let them fall. The goal
   is to identify where you've lost your momentum and been hurt so you
   can specifically give it to God and watch Him bring healing there.

3. Ask the Holy Spirit to show you one small step that will help you get
   your hope and your vision back. Write it out. Share it with someone
   you trust and ask them to believe with you for renewal in this area —
   and be willing to do the same for them.

TOPIC

Faith and Patience: A Marriage That Produces Results

SCRIPTURES

1. **Hebrews 6:12** — That ye be not slothful, but followers of them who through faith and patience inherit the promises.

2. **Revelation 3:15,16** — I know thy works, that thou art neither cold nor hot: I would thou wert cold or hot. So then because thou art luke-warm, and neither cold nor hot, I will spue thee out of my mouth.

3. **Hebrews 10:36** — For ye have need of patience, that, after ye have done the will of God, ye might receive the promise.

4. **Galatians 6:9** — And let us not be weary in well doing: for in due season we shall reap, if we faint not.

5. **Habakkuk 2:2,3** — And the Lord answered me, and said, Write the vision, and make it plain upon tables, that he may run that readeth it. For the vision is yet for an appointed time, but at the end it shall speak, and not lie: though it tarry, wait for it; because it will surely come, it will not tarry.

6. **Hebrews 10:23** — Let us hold fast the profession of our faith without wavering; (for he is faithful that promised).

7. **Philippians 1:6** — Being confident of this very thing, that he which hath begun a good work in you will perform it until the day of Jesus Christ.

GREEK WORDS

1. "slothful" — νωθρός (*nothros*): slow and sluggish; something that has lost its speed or momentum; conveying the idea of something that has lost the drive, thrust, impetus, pace, and speed it once possessed; the idea of one whose zeal has now dissipated; denotes a person who has become disinterested and whose zeal has been replaced with a middle-of-the-road, take-it-or-leave-it mentality; it carries the idea of

one who has a lethargic, lackadaisical, apathetic, indifferent, lukewarm attitude toward life; a non-achiever or non-achieving attitude

2. "need" — χρεία (*chreia*): a lack, deficit, shortage

3. "patience" — ὑπομονή (*hupomone*): to stay or to abide; to remain in one's spot; to keep a position; to resolve to maintain territory that has been gained; in a military sense, pictures soldiers who were ordered to maintain their positions even in the face of fierce combat; to defiantly stick it out, regardless of the pressure mounted against it; endurance; staying power; "hang-in-there" power; the attitude that holds out, holds on, outlasts, perseveres, and hangs in there, never giving up, refusing to surrender to obstacles, and turning down every opportunity to quit; pictures one under a heavy load, but who refuses to bend, break, or surrender because he is convinced that the territory, promise, or principle under assault rightfully belongs to him; stamina, durability

4. "receive" — κομίζω (*komidzo*): receive; to receive what is due; to receive what one has coming to him

5. "through" — διά (*dia*): indicates instrumentality

6. "weary" — ἐνκακῶμεν (*enkakomen*): to give in or to surrender to that which is bad or evil

7. "faint" — ἐκλύω (*ekluo*): to faint; to let go; to loosen up; to relax; to lose altogether; to release; to surrender; to grow weary; to give up; the image of one who relinquishes his grip on an object or principle because of exhaustion, exasperation, or weariness; a relaxed mental state that results in loss; depicts one so weary that he gives up and forfeits what he had long awaited

8. "hold fast" — κατέχω (*katecho*): a compound of κατα (*kata*) and ἔχω (*echo*); the preposition κατα (*kata*) carries the idea of something that comes downward or something that comes down so hard and heavily that it is overpowering, dominating, and even subjugating, thus, something that conquers, subdues, and immediately begins to demonstrate its overwhelming, influencing power; the word ἔχω (*echo*) means "I have" and carries the idea of possession; when compounded, the word doesn't just mean to embrace, it actually means to embrace something tightly, and because of the preposition *kata*, it is the image of someone who finds the object of his dreams and then holds it down — even to the point of sitting on it — in order to dominate and take control of it; to suppress

9. "wavering" — κλίνω (*klino*): to bow down, to slope the shoulders, to bend over, or to go to bed; to give up, to yield, to bend, to give ground to; it can also be translated as bed or pallet

SYNOPSIS

As you stand on your word from God and resolve to do all you need to do to fulfill the divine assignment God has given you, you need to be aware of another extremely sinister and sneaky enemy that will try to steal the dream from your heart. This wicked foe doesn't come from the devil, nor does it necessarily come from your environment, your friends, or your families. This wretched enemy comes from you — your flesh. It is dream thief number five, which we introduced in our last lesson: *neutrality*.

Although you may not want to hear it, the greatest enemy you'll have to overcome in your life is *you*. Your flesh — which is all that you are apart from God — has a mind of its own. What your flesh wants, thinks, and feels is constantly at war with what the Holy Spirit knows is right and best for your life. If you learn how to overcome your flesh, which includes the insidious trap of neutrality, you can do anything that God will ever ask you to do.

The emphasis of this lesson:

Faith and patience are two instruments we need to inherit God's promises. Patience is the womb in which the seeds of faith are sown to give birth to the dream God has placed in our hearts. Faith alone cannot produce the promises of God. We need patience to endure the time of waiting until we enter the season of harvest. If we don't grow weary or faint, we will most certainly reap what God promised.

What Does It Mean To Be 'Slothful'?

So far, we've examined five dream thieves that come to steal the dream God has placed in our hearts. The first four are *time, Satan, friends*, and *family*, and the fifth one, which we introduced in our last lesson, is neutrality. This fifth dream thief is a subtle enemy lurking in the shadows that often goes undetected. If you're not careful, it will worm its way into your life and overtake you without your even being aware of its presence. It is referred to in Hebrews 6:12, which says, "…Be not slothful, but followers of them who through faith and patience inherit the promises."

As we noted in Lesson 6, the word "slothful" is the Greek word *nothros*, which is from where we get the word *neutral*. It means *to be slow and sluggish* and describes *something that has lost its speed or momentum*. It conveys the idea of *something that has lost the drive, thrust, impetus, pace, and speed it once possessed*. It is a picture of *one whose zeal has now dissipated* and denotes *a person who has become disinterested and whose zeal has been replaced with a middle-of-the-road, take-it-or-leave-it mentality*. Moreover, it carries the idea of *one who has a lethargic, lackadaisical, apathetic, indifferent, or lukewarm attitude toward life*. Thus, this person is *a non-achiever* or has a *non-achieving attitude*.

In this passage, "slothful" does not mean being lazy or inactive. This person may be doing a lot of things, but inwardly they've become neutralized and have lost their momentum and passion for God. A classic example of this condition is the church of Laodicea which Jesus addressed in Revelation 3:15 and 16. Out of deep love and compassion, He said:

> **I know thy works, that thou art neither cold nor hot: I would thou wert cold or hot. So then because thou art lukewarm, and neither cold nor hot, I will spue thee out of my mouth.**

Now, you may read this and think, *Being cold sounds worse than being lukewarm. Why would Jesus say He wished they were hot **or** cold? That's a bit confusing*. To help you understand what Jesus is really saying, let's review the history of the city of Laodicea.

Water Was an Issue in Laodicea

Laodicea was located on a hill in the very center of the Lycus Valley. As wealthy as this city was, it had no natural water source. Interestingly, just a short distance to the south was the city of Colossae, which was known for its cold, refreshing waters that came down from the top of the mountains. It was actually a resort city, and during the summer months, people went there to refresh themselves.

At the same time, just to the north of Laodicea was the city of Hierapolis, which was famous for its hot mineral springs. People would journey there regularly to bathe in those springs because they were therapeutic and promoted healing. Not having their own water source, the Laodicean leaders and citizens decided to use their vast riches and build a pipeline to transport both hot and cold water from these neighboring cities into their town. Thus, they constructed the first engineered system of pipes in the history of the world.

Needless to say, the Laodiceans were very excited about their great achievement. Unfortunately, by the time the cold water made its way from Colossae to Laodicea, it had lost its coldness and was no longer refreshing. Likewise, by the time the hot water made it to Laodicea from Hierapolis, it had decreased in temperature and lost its healing properties. What the townspeople were left with was lukewarm water that was neither cold and refreshing nor hot and therapeutic.

What made matters worse was the fact that the pipes were made from clay that was filled with minerals, and by the time the water arrived in Laodicea, it had a putrid taste because of all the minerals that had dissolved in it. When the people in Laodicea tasted it, it failed their expectations. In fact, the water was so sickening they spit it out.

Lukewarmness Is a Deadly Disorder

Can you see why Jesus compared the Laodicean believers to distasteful, lukewarm water? It was an analogy they could all easily grasp. Essentially, Jesus was telling them — and *us* — He would rather that we be cold and refreshing or hot and therapeutic in our relation to Him and others. If we are lukewarm, it is extremely distasteful — even sickening — to Jesus, and it makes Him want to spit us out of His mouth. Although this doesn't mean that we lose our salvation, it does mean that being lukewarm (or *neutral*) is quite repulsive to Jesus.

Neutrality — or being *lukewarm* — is a serious condition. Hebrews 6:12 calls it "slothfulness" — the Greek word *nothros* — and it could be typified by a candle that once burned brightly but whose dim flame doesn't shine like it once did. It could also describe a person who once felt very deeply about a certain goal and was wholeheartedly committed to achieving it — but whose passion is no longer what it once was.

Previously this person put all his time, effort, and attention into that cause, but now he doesn't even seem to care about it. His commitment to the dream has become slack, and his passion has begun to wear off. All these descriptions provide an accurate portrayal of the Greek word *nothros*.

To sum it up, neutrality — *nothros* — is a picture of:

- *Something that is neither hot nor cold.*

- *Someone who is neither committed nor uncommitted.*

- *An attitude or mentality that really couldn't care less anymore.*

A person in this condition has lost his zeal, his passion, and his conviction for the vision or goal that once burned so brightly in his heart.

We All Have 'Need of Patience'

Looking once more at Hebrews 10:36, it says, "For ye have need of patience, that, after ye have done the will of God, ye might receive the promise" (Hebrews 10:36). If you stop and think about it, the reason people move out of drive and into neutral is that they get tired of waiting and waiting for their dream to come to pass. As we noted earlier, the word "need" in this verse is the Greek word *chreia*, which denotes *a lack, deficit,* or *shortage*. All of us have a deficit or shortage of "patience."

In Greek, this word "patience" is *hupomone*, which was considered by the Early Church to be the queen of all virtues. They believed that if you had patience, you would always win. It wasn't a matter of *if* you would win, but *when* you would win. The word *endurance* would be a great word to sum up the meaning of the word "patience."

Keep in mind that "patience" — the Greek word *hupomone* — is a compound of the word *hupo*, meaning *under*, and the word *meno*, meaning *to stay* or *to abide*. When compounded, the word *hupomone*, means *to stay or to abide; to remain in one's spot*; or *to keep a position*. It indicates *a resolve to maintain territory that has been gained*. In a military sense, it pictures soldiers who were ordered to maintain their positions even in the face of fierce combat.

Furthermore, this word *hupomone* (patience) means *to defiantly stick it out regardless of the pressure mounted against it*. It expresses the idea of *endurance; staying power*; or *"hang-in-there" power*. It is *the attitude that holds out, holds on, outlasts, perseveres, and hangs in there, never giving up, refusing to surrender to obstacles, and turning down every opportunity to quit*. This word "patience" is a picture of one who is under a heavy load but refuses to bend, break, or surrender because he is convinced that the territory, promise, or principle under assault rightfully belongs to him. The word *hupomone* (patience) can also describe *stamina* or *durability*.

Again, the writer of Hebrews says, "For ye have need of patience, that, after ye have done the will of God, ye might receive the promise" (Hebrews

10:36). The word "receive" in Greek is *komidzo*, which literally means *to receive what is due* or *to receive what one has coming to him*. Thus, whatever God has promised you is exactly what you're going to receive. Your *recompense* or *reward* is on its way to you — as long as you don't give up.

Faith and Patience Are Required To Produce God's Promises

After the Bible tells us not to be slothful — *neutral* — it goes on to make this vital statement: "…Through faith and patience [we] inherit the promises" (Hebrews 6:12). The word "through" here is the Greek word *dia*, which indicates *instrumentality*. The use of this word tells us that faith and patience are two *instruments* that we need to inherit God's promises.

To a degree, these two are like a husband and wife — both are needed to produce a child. Although some people will say, "All you need is faith to receive God's promises," that is not true. Just as a man cannot produce a child on his own, neither can faith produce the promises of God without patience. How ridiculous would it be for a woman to say, "I'm going to have a baby all by myself." It just can't happen.

In the same way the man provides seed to sow into the woman, faith is the seed sown into the womb of patience. The two work together to give birth to the promises of God. Here again, the word "patience" is the Greek word *hupomone*, which describes *endurance*, *stamina*, *durability*, and the divine ability *to stay put and hang in there* until the promised desired is obtained. The Bible — especially Hebrews 11 — is filled with examples of individuals who received a word from God, but that word took a great deal of time to become a reality. Each person had to have patience as they waited for their "due season" to harvest God's word to them.

This leads us to Galatians 6:9, which says, "And let us not be weary in well doing: for in due season we shall reap, if we faint not." The word "weary" is the plural word *enkakomen*, a compound of the word *en*, meaning *in*, and *kakomen*, which describes *evil*. When these words are compounded to form *enkakomen*, it means *to give in or to surrender to that which is evil or bad*. This tells us that when we give up and walk away from what God told us to do, He views our actions as being *evil*.

The word "faint" in this passage is a translation of the Greek word *ekluo*, which is a compound of the words *ek* and *luo*. The word *ek* means *out*, and the word *lou* means *to loosen*. When these words are joined to form *ekluo*, it means *to faint; to let go; to loosen up; to relax; to lose altogether; to release; to surrender; to grow weary*, or *to give up*. It is the image of *one who relinquishes his grip on an object or principle because of exhaustion, exasperation, or weariness*. Moreover, it depicts *a relaxed mental state that results in loss or one so weary that he gives up and forfeits what he had long awaited*.

Friend, don't surrender to the urge to quit, and don't let neutrality paralyze you. Keep sowing your faith into patience and wait for the promise of God to become a reality. Scripture says, "…For in due season we shall reap, if we faint not" (Galatians 6:9). That's God's promise!

What God Says, He Does

In many ways, the phrase "in due time" is much like "an appointed time." That's what the Holy Spirit prompted the prophet Habakkuk to write about. In Habakkuk 2:2 and 3, the Bible says, "And the Lord answered me, and said, Write the vision, and make it plain upon tables, that he may run that readeth it. For the vision is yet for *an appointed time*, but at the end it shall speak, and not lie: though it tarry, wait for it; because it will surely come, it will not tarry."

The words "an appointed time" indicate that the vision or dream God gave us doesn't come to pass in a day or two. After He gives it, it may not happen the next week, the next month, or even the next year. The vision will take place at "an appointed time." Although it seems to tarry or be delayed, God says we are to wait for it. "Don't give up!" He urges us. "Endure — be patient — because it will surely come to pass."

Remember, "God is not a man, that He should lie, nor a son of man, that He should repent. Has He said, and will He not do? Or has He spoken, and will He not make it good?" (Numbers 23:19 *NKJV*) In other words, what God says He's going to do is precisely what He will do. He just needs you to embrace the word, the call, the dream that He gave you and stand by it till it comes to pass.

That is why He urges us to "…hold fast the profession of our faith without wavering…" (Hebrews 10:23). In Greek, the word for "wavering" is *klino*, which means *to bow down, to slope the shoulders, to bend over*, or *to go to bed*. It pictures a person who gives up, yields, bends, or gives ground to another. What's interesting is that it is the New Testament word for *a bed or pallet a person sleeps on*. The use of the word *klino* indicates that if you don't hold on to the dream God gave you, you'll end up bent over, exhausted, and going to bed on your faith.

Always remember, "…He [God] is faithful that promised" (Hebrews 10:23). Paul reiterated this truth in Philippians 1:6, saying, "Being confident of this very thing, that he which hath begun a good work in you will perform it until the day of Jesus Christ." Friend, your "due season" is on its way! Don't give up or give in. Continue to stand in faith until the promises of God become a reality in your life.

STUDY QUESTIONS

Study to shew thyself approved unto God, a workman that needeth not to be ashamed, rightly dividing the word of truth.
— 2 Timothy 2:15

1. What new facts stood out to you about the city of Laodicea? How did these details help you better understand Jesus' words in Revelation 3 about being lukewarm?

2. The "appointed time" when a dream comes to pass is definitely not in our control, which can make it incredibly hard to keep hoping — especially if we've been waiting for years or even decades. What does Scripture tell us to do when we feel overwhelmed? (*See* Matthew 11:28-30; Hebrews 4:15,16; Psalm 61:1-5.) What can we remember about God's perspective and plans for us that will help us hold on and not give up? (*See* Isaiah 55:8-9; First Corinthians 13:12; Jeremiah 29:11; and Psalm 139.)

3. Numbers 23:19 asks and answers the question we all have sometimes: *Will God actually do what He says He will do?* What else does Scripture say about the reliability of His Word and the certainty we can have that His promises will come to pass? (*See* Isaiah 55:10,11; Matthew 24:35; Joshua 21:45; and First Kings 8:56.)

PRACTICAL APPLICATION

But be ye doers of the word, and not hearers only, deceiving your own selves.
— James 1:22

Go back and reflect on the meaning of the Greek word for "patience" (*hupomone*) It creates a picture of assured victory...*if we'll just keep going.* It's like a game of tug-of-war where God has guaranteed you that the opposing team WILL let go at some point, and if you're still holding on when they do, you'll win.

1.   What rope (or ropes) have you gotten tired of tugging? Is it integrity? Sexual purity? Vulnerability? Hope? Belief in God's goodness? Or something else?

2.   When did you first notice yourself starting to get tired? Whenever it was, ask the Holy Spirit to give you the *grace* you need to stay in the game (*see* Psalm 84:11; James 4:6). He has all the strength you need, and He wants to give it to you!

3.   Not long after God called Abraham, He made him a promise that he would be a father of many nations. Immediately, Abraham responded to God by building Him an altar and worshipping Him (*see* Genesis 12:7,8.) Building an altar represents something that we can do even today that will reinforce our faith like nothing else — what is it? (*Consider* Deuteronomy 8:2; Psalm 77:11,12; First Chronicles 16:11,12; and First Corinthians 11:23-26.)

LESSON 8

TOPIC

Taking Steps To Fulfill Your Dream

SCRIPTURES

1.   **1 Kings 19:19-21** — So he [Elijah] departed thence, and found Elisha the son of Shaphat, who was plowing with twelve yoke of oxen before him, and he with the twelfth: and Elijah passed by him, and cast his mantle upon him. And he left the oxen, and ran after Elijah, and said, Let me, I pray thee, kiss my father and my mother, and then I will follow thee.... And he returned back from him, and took a yoke of oxen, and slew them, and boiled their flesh with the instruments of the oxen, and gave unto the people, and they did eat. Then he arose, and went after Elijah, and ministered unto him.

2. **Luke 14:16-20** — Then said he unto him, A certain man made a
    great supper, and bade many: and sent his servant at supper time to
    say to them that were bidden, Come; for all things are now ready. And
    they all with one consent began to make excuse. The first said unto
    him, I have bought a piece of ground, and I must needs go and see
    it: I pray thee have me excused. And another said, I have bought five
    yoke of oxen, and I go to prove them: I pray thee have me excused.
    And another said, I have married a wife, and therefore I cannot come.

GREEK WORDS

There are no Greek words in this lesson.

SYNOPSIS

The call of God rarely comes at a convenient moment. Rather, it usually
comes when you're in the middle of doing something else or when you've
already made other plans. Then suddenly God speaks to your heart, and you
are jarred into facing the reality that He's asking you to do something you
hadn't previously considered or thought about. From that moment forward,
you start trying to figure out how to get from where you are to where you
need to be in order to accomplish what God is asking you to do.

For example, you may wonder: *What about my house payments? What about
my job? What about my current commitments? What about my credit-card debt
and the other bills that I need to pay? What about my relationships? How will
this decision affect those around me? What about my elderly parents? How will
God's call on my life change my availability to them?*

These are all normal questions that arise in your mind when the reality of
God's call begins to fully dawn on you. It's at that point you need to know
what steps to take next and how to release yourself from your current
commitments so you can follow the dream God has placed in your heart.

The emphasis of this lesson:

**God doesn't call those that are just sitting around waiting for some-
thing to happen — He calls those who are actively doing something. If
you prove yourself faithful, God will entrust you with more. But before
you step out to obey His call, you'll need to detach yourself from what
you're currently doing. This includes taking care of family and financial**

responsibilities. **Doing things right the first time is the smartest, least expensive, and best way to live.**

When We First Receive God's Calling It Is Often Sudden, Unexpected, and Jarring

When you study the lives of God's people in the Old and New Testament, the call of God usually came to individuals who were already very busy doing other things. Noah, Abraham, and Moses are all examples of this fact. Few people in Scripture exemplify how the call of God comes on a person more profoundly than Elisha. The account of his calling is found in First Kings 19:19-21.

Verse 19 says, "So he [Elijah] departed thence, and found Elisha the son of Shaphat, who was plowing with twelve yoke of oxen before him, and he with the twelfth: and Elijah passed by him, and cast his mantle upon him." Isn't it interesting that when the prophetic mantle of God first came to Elisha, he wasn't in his prayer closet praying about his future ministry. On the contrary, he was out busily plowing the field with twelve yokes of oxen. That tells us a great deal about the stage of his life when the call of God came to him. He was actively laboring in his profession, and the fact that he had twelve yokes of oxen means he was very successful at what he was doing.

When God asks a person to do something he's never done before, it's natural for him to wonder if he's equipped to do the job. It's normal for him to pray, *Lord, are You sure You're choosing the right guy?* Countless millions have asked this question — maybe you have too. The primary reason people don't step out and obey what God is telling them to do is that they are afraid to take that big leap of faith.

God Calls People Who Are Active and Faithful

When the call of God first came to Elisha, he was already very busy with what he was doing. His occupation was clearly defined, and he had become very good at it. In fact, the Bible tells us that Elisha was so committed to his business, he was *yoked* to his team of oxen. This is symbolic of the state his life was in at the time.

Notice the Bible is careful to say Elisha had "twelve yoke," or 12 pairs, of oxen. In biblical times, oxen were very expensive. They were the tractors and the plows of that day, and very few farmers were wealthy enough to own 24 oxen, which is why the Holy Spirit included this fact in Scripture. Twenty-four oxen represented very big money, which means Elisha was no small-time farmer. He was very successful and huge in the farming business.

It was when Elisha had this successful business, being both very busy and good at what he was doing, that God suddenly called him. There are several things that we can learn from this, but listen carefully to these points, because many people don't grasp what you're about to read — and that's why they are unsuccessful in their lives, businesses, and ministries.

For starters, people often get the impression that God calls those that are just sitting around waiting for something to happen. They have a "pie in the sky" mentality and think that one day out of the clear blue, a lightning bolt is going to strike them from Heaven. Then suddenly out of nowhere, they're going to be propelled forward into a big change — that somehow they're going to be catapulted into a fabulous, phenomenal life. But this kind of thinking borders on hallucination.

You can search the Bible, and you won't find one person significantly used by God who was lazily doing nothing when the call of God came to him or her. Just like Elisha, all the people God called were actively doing something else when He spoke to them. Think about it — why would God want to call someone to do *His* work when that person hasn't successfully done his or her *own* work?

The People God Chose Were Successful *Before* They Answered His Call

God is watching us, and everything we're doing right now is a time of qualification to see if we're ready for the next assignment He has prepared for us. He is looking to see if we're busy and faithfully doing the last thing He told us to do. This is true of nearly everyone God called in Scripture. Here are a few strategic, well-known, key Bible characters who were already successful *before* God called them:

- *Noah* was successful and righteous before God called him to build the ark.

- *Abraham* was successful and rich before God called him to become the father of His covenant people.

- *Joshua* was successful as Moses' associate before God called him to be the leader of Israel.

- *David* was successful as a shepherd before God called him to be the next king of Israel.

- *Daniel* was successful in Nebuchadnezzar's court and walked in integrity before God called him to be one of His prophets.

- *Matthew* was successful as a tax collector before Jesus called him to follow Him.

- *Peter* was a successful fisherman and businessman before Jesus called him to be His disciple.

- *Luke* was a successful doctor before he was called into the ministry.

- *Paul* was a successful politician and religious leader before God called him into apostolic ministry.

- *Timothy* was successful as Paul's associate and disciple before he became the pastor of the church of Ephesus.

The fact that God called these people who were already faithful and successful in what they were doing confirms what Jesus said in Matthew 25:29: "For unto every one that hath shall be given, and he shall have abundance: but from him that hath not shall be taken away even that which he hath." This passage clearly states that how you perform *right now* may be the factor that determines whether God will call you to do something greater and more significant later. If you prove yourself faithful, God will know He can trust you with the next promotion.

Dealing With Family and Financial Commitments *First* Is a Must

Before you ever step out to obey God's call, you need to learn how to detach yourself from what you're currently doing. To go from where you are to where God wants you to be, you have to become unhitched from many of your present responsibilities, commitments, and even some relationships. For example, if you have a car payment or house payment, you have to know how you're going to make your payments or become released from them.

Sadly, many believers have stepped out to answer God's call prematurely — *before* they dealt with important issues such as these. Rick and Denise saw this personally when they first moved their family to the Soviet Union. Although the hearts of the missionaries were right, and they really wanted to obey God, some didn't take the necessary steps of preparation to do what God was asking.

For instance, there were missionaries who left the United States and moved to the former Soviet Union *before* they knew how they were going to pay their bills or how they were going to care for their elderly parents. They made multiple sacrifices in order to get to the geographic location God had called them, but they couldn't stay because they had not become unyoked from various responsibilities back home.

Realize that obeying God never means that we can ignore our family and abandon our finances for someone else to have to deal with. That is a lack of integrity, and it is irresponsible. People are important to God and must be handled with honor, respect, and love. Finances are also important and must be managed responsibly.

Yes, it may take a little longer to do things right the first time, but nothing is as difficult as abandoning your call to go back and fix what should have been done right in the beginning. Doing things right the first time is the smartest, least expensive, and best way to live.

Never forget that when Jesus was dying on the Cross, He had His mother Mary on His mind. The Bible says while He was hanging there bearing the sins and sicknesses of the world upon Himself, He looked down at her standing next to the young apostle John and said, "...Woman, behold thy son!" (John 19:26). He then looked to John and said, "...Behold thy mother!" Verse 27 continues, "And from that hour that disciple took her unto his own home" (John 19:27).

Interestingly, in the very next verse, the Bible says, "After this, Jesus knowing that all things were now accomplished..." (v. 28). The moment Jesus knew the care of His mother was entrusted into John's hands, He knew everything was taken care of — including His family responsibilities. Think about it — Jesus was departing the earth to become our Great High Priest. Yet He took time to make sure His mother's care was secured. It was that important to Him.

Elisha Is an Example of Radical Obedience

Once you know what God's call is, you must take the necessary steps to deal with all family and financial commitments honorably and responsibly, making sure you won't need to turn around again to have to address unfinished business. That is what we see Elisha doing before he began serving as Elijah's apprentice.

As soon as Elijah threw his mantle upon Elisha, Elisha said, "...Let me, I pray thee, kiss my father and my mother, and then I will follow thee..." (1 Kings 19:20). Clearly, Elisha had feelings for his family and wanted to personally express his love to them. He didn't want to leave any details back home undone or neglected. By taking the needed steps he took, he was able to move forward with the call of God on his life with peace in his heart.

The thing that Elisha did next shows the depth of his commitment. The Bible says, "And he returned back from him, and took a yoke of oxen, and slew them, and boiled their flesh with the instruments of the oxen, and gave unto the people, and they did eat. Then he arose, and went after Elijah, and ministered unto him" (1 Kings 19:21).

Think carefully about what Elisha did in front of his family. First, he killed his oxen, which were the expensive engines of his farming business that drove his plowing and planting equipment. Next, he took the wooden apparatus that held the oxen together and that they pulled through the soil, and he broke it into pieces to light on fire. He then took the oxen, cooked them on the fire, and fed the food to his family and friends. In doing so, he was publicly burning every bridge behind him and sending a signal to his family, his friends, and even to himself that this was *the point of no return.*

What do you think Elisha felt as he watched the blood oozing from his oxen he had just killed? What do you think went through his mind as he heard the popping and crackling sounds of the wooden equipment burning in the blazing fire?

In that moment, when that equipment and the oxen went up in smoke, Elisha was saying goodbye to the life he had known. His decision had been made, and there was no turning back. His obedience to God was radical, and for you to do what God is asking you to do, you will have to be radical in your obedience too.

Don't Let the Cares of This World Devour Your Dream

While it's important and right for us to take care of our responsibilities, we can't allow them to keep us from accepting and walking out the call of God on our life. Jesus addresses this in a parable He told in Luke 14:16-20:

> **Then said he unto him, A certain man made a great supper, and bade many: and sent his servant at supper time to say to them that were bidden, Come; for all things are now ready. And they all with one consent began to make excuse. The first said unto him, I have bought a piece of ground, and I must needs go and see it: I pray thee have me excused. And another said, I have bought five yoke of oxen, and I go to prove them: I pray thee have me excused. And another said, I have married a wife, and therefore I cannot come.**

All these people who had been invited to the banquet made excuses for why they couldn't accept the invitation and attend. They were so entangled with the natural things of this life that they just couldn't let them go and embrace what the "certain man" — who represents God — was asking them to do. If you think about it, the things these individuals felt they needed to deal with are the same things we deal with today: buying and taking care of property; managing business responsibilities (which are represented by the oxen); and taking care of our spouse and family.

Although we must be faithful and responsible in all these areas, we can't let any of them become a noose around our necks that paralyzes us and keeps us from pursuing the dream God has given us. Once we know God's plan, there is nothing more important than that. If we settle for what we are currently doing when we know there's something else we're supposed to do, we'll always wonder, *What would have happened had I obeyed?* It was this very thought that hounded Rick and brought him to the place where he obeyed God and moved his family to the Soviet Union.

That's a question you need to ask yourself: *What will I miss if I don't obey God?* Another question of equal importance would be, *What will my children and spouse miss if I don't obey?* Realize God has amazing and wonderful things planned for you and your loved ones, but to experience those blessings, you must obey His leading.

Friend, continue to work diligently and faithfully on what God has already called you to do. Once you know and understand the new thing He's asking you to do, take the needed steps to responsibly deal with what you need to address before stepping out. Make every effort to express love to your family members and take care of your elderly parents if necessary. Devise a plan to make good on debts that you owe and detach from any financial commitments that you can. Then put your whole heart and soul into doing what God has told you to do. He will honor and reward your actions of obedience as you pursue your dream!

STUDY QUESTIONS

> **Study to shew thyself approved unto God, a workman that needeth not to be ashamed, rightly dividing the word of truth.**
> **— 2 Timothy 2:15**

1. Like Elisha, another remarkable man in the Old Testament was hard at work when God approached him with a calling that seemed bigger-than-life. Who was he? What was he doing at the time? Where was God calling him to go? How did God confirm to him that he was moving in the right direction? (*See* Judges 6.)

2. As Gideon was in the midst of preparing for a battle, he gathered as many soldiers as he could muster in order to ensure victory against Midian. What instructions did God give him after he was finished amassing his army? (*See* Judges 7:2-8.) Why do you think He told Gideon to do something that made so little logical sense? How did God prove yet again that Gideon was on the right track? (*See* Judges 7:9-15.)

PRACTICAL APPLICATION

> **But be ye doers of the word, and not hearers only, deceiving your own selves.**
> **— James 1:22**

1. What part of what God has called you to do feels too big for you? What is a "fleece" that comes to mind that you can ask God to give you to confirm that you heard Him accurately? Take a moment to pray and ask Him to give you the assurance you need to take your next step of faith.

2. In Jesus' parable of the banquet, the host of the party wanted more than anything to see his home filled with guests enjoying themselves. Sadly, many of his invitees made excuses regarding their responsibilities that kept them from experiencing the good things he had for them. What is an *empty* activity that you find yourself repeatedly involved in? Is it something God has asked you to do or a task you took upon yourself that you feel obligated to do? What kind of fruit is it producing in your life?

3. Take a moment to invite the Holy Spirit to show you how you can start to lay down all lifeless and unnecessary activities and pick up the mantle of your genuine calling. The closeness He wants to have with you is priceless. Journal what He says.

4. Stop and take an honest look at where you are in life right now. How are you doing? Are you actively accomplishing the last thing God called you to do? Ask yourself some simple questions like:

   - *Am I giving it 100 percent of my effort?*

   - *Do I finish projects, or do I bail out and leave things incomplete?*

   - *Can I be trusted with money? Do I operate in integrity?*

   - *Would I want to hire someone with an attitude like mine?*

   - *Does my life and attitude reflect the qualities that would make God want to choose me for a bigger, more significant assignment?*

5. Considering your answers from Question 4, what things in your life need to change? Is there anything you need to repent of and ask for God's forgiveness? Take a few minutes to pray and be honest with Him. Ask Him to show you what adjustments you need to make and to give you the grace (strength) you need to make them.

TOPIC

A Threefold Cord Is Not Easily Broken

SCRIPTURES

1. **Ecclesiastes 4:9-12** — Two are better than one; because they have a good reward for their labour. For if they fall, the one will lift up his fellow: but woe to him that is alone when he falleth; for he hath not another to help him up. Again, if two lie together, then they have heat: but how can one be warm alone? And if one prevail against him, two shall withstand him; and a threefold cord is not quickly broken.

2. **Matthew 18:19** — Again I say unto you, That if two of you shall agree on earth as touching any thing that they shall ask, it shall be done for them of my Father which is in heaven.

3. **Galatians 6:2** — Bear ye one another's burdens, and so fulfil the law of Christ.

4. **Psalm 20:2** (*NIV*) — May he send you help from the sanctuary and grant you support from Zion.

5. **Hebrews 10:24,25** — And let us consider one another to provoke unto love and to good works: not forsaking the assembling of ourselves together, as the manner of some is; but exhorting one another: and so much the more, as ye see the day approaching.

6. **Proverbs 17:17** — A friend loveth at all times, and a brother is born for adversity.

7. **Hebrews 3:13** — But exhort one another daily, while it is called To day; lest any of you be hardened through the deceitfulness of sin.

8. **Hebrews 10:23** — Let us hold fast the profession of our faith without wavering; (for he is faithful that promised).

GREEK WORDS

1. "burdens" — βάρος (*baros*): a weight that is heavy or crushing; a crushing weight; could refer to either a physical problem, circumstan-

tial problem, or spiritual problem; a burden too heavy to carry alone; if one attempts to carry it alone, it would be crushing to bear

2. "consider" — κατανοέω (*katanoeo*): to thoroughly consider; to think something through from the top to the bottom; to deeply ponder; pictures a person engaged in focused and concentrated consideration; presents the idea of mulling something over; to carefully contemplate; to ponder and carefully look at a particular issue; to examine and fully study a subject

3. "provoke" — παροξυσμός (*paroxusmos*): prodding a person to do something; to call into combat; to irritate, to incite, to anger, to inflame, or to enrage; to provoke

SYNOPSIS

As you begin to take steps to make your dream a reality, God will place other people in your life to assist you. He brings these relationships into your life for the purpose of encouraging and provoking you to respond correctly as difficult situations arise. As much as you may not want to hear it, it is a guarantee that difficult situations *will* arise, because the enemy will try to stop God's plan from being fulfilled in your life.

We call these difficulties dream thieves, and there are two fundamental reasons why we give in to the tactics of dream thieves and forsake our vision. The first involves our individual walk with the Lord. We must guard our hearts and minds by spending time in the Word and praying for divine guidance and strength from the Holy Spirit. The second reason we lose our passion and abandon our dream concerns our relationships within the Body of Christ.

Sometimes after much time has passed since we've received our word or dream from God, we can begin carrying an enormous burden of discouragement and fail to turn to other believers for help and support. Left unchecked, *isolation* sets in — which is dream thief number six. Make no mistake — God never intended for us to live our lives of faith alone. We need each other as we endeavor to carry out the dreams He gives us.

The emphasis of this lesson:

God created us for community — not isolation. The Bible says a three-fold cord — which is you, your godly friend, and God — is not quickly broken. We are called to carefully study each other and learn how to

motivate one another to move in the right direction. Likewise, we're to help carry the weight of those burdens that are too heavy for us to bear alone. With the strength of fellow believers, we are empowered to endure and hold fast to our faith until we receive the manifestation of God's promise.

There's Power in a 'Threefold Cord'

A person who willfully chooses to do life alone has succumbed to the dream thief of *isolation*. If the enemy can succeed in isolating us from other brothers and sisters in Christ, he can stop our spiritual growth in its tracks and make it nearly impossible for us to fulfill our divine destiny. How does he do it? He feeds us lies such as:

- *No one really likes me.*

- *No one has ever had the problem or weakness I struggle with.*

- *No one would like me if I ever opened up and shared who I really am.*

- *What do I have to offer anyone anyway?*

- *It's better and safer for me to stay to myself and not let anyone get too close to me.*

It's lies like these that cause people to retreat within themselves, hiding themselves away until they are fully isolated and alone.

Another common cause of isolation occurs when believers become offended or hurt by other believers and then use those offenses, which have left them with a broken heart, as excuses to withdraw from all believers. These offended individuals decide in their minds that all Christians are exactly like the person who mistreated or hurt them. Consequently, they often turn away from the Church and pursue friendships in the world instead.

Isolation isn't just a matter of physically distancing yourself from fellowship with other believers or from those in spiritual authority or from attending church. You can be in the midst of a thriving church congregation every week and still be in isolation by disengaging and detaching yourself emotionally and spiritually from those around you. As a result, you miss out on receiving the supply of strength and encouragement that fellow believers provide.

Please realize that to allow yourself to become isolated and separated from the rest of the Body of Christ or from those in spiritual authority for ANY reason can be deadly to your walk with God and to the ultimate fulfillment of your dream. Instead of healing one's pain, isolation makes the problem worse. The fact is that your faith and your ability to endure can suffer tremendously if you live in isolation and disconnected from the Church. Without the strength of fellow believers, it is more difficult to endure and hold fast to your faith until you receive the manifestation of God's promise.

What's the answer to this debilitating dilemma? Invest time in developing healthy relationships. Look at what Solomon, the wisest man of his day, had to say about the value of friends:

> **Two are better than one; because they have a good reward for their labour. For if they fall, the one will lift up his fellow: but woe to him that is alone when he falleth; for he hath not another to help him up. Again, if two lie together, then they have heat: but how can one be warm alone? And if one prevail against him, two shall withstand him; and a threefold cord is not quickly broken.**
>
> **— Ecclesiastes 4:9-12**

The "threefold cord" Solomon is talking about is *you, your godly friend*, and *God*. Even Jesus needed the fellowship of friends. In His time of temptation in the Garden of Gethsemane, He took His three closest disciples to pray with Him because He needed their strength and encouragement. Jesus said, "…That if two of you shall agree on earth as touching any thing that they shall ask, it shall be done for them of my Father which is in heaven" (Matthew 18:19). This shows the power of agreement. Sure, you can pray by yourself, but the release of God's power grows exponentially when you come together in agreement with others.

We Are To Help 'Bear One Another's Burdens'

Now, it's important to note that when the Bible talks about and encourages relationships, it is not referring to *co-dependency*, which is an abnormal reliance on another person, making that individual the source of their strength and life instead of Jesus Christ. As believers, we must find the biblical balance for godly relationships.

Consider what the apostle Paul says in Galatians 6:2: "Bear ye one another's burdens, and so fulfil the law of Christ." The word "burdens" here is the Greek word *baros*, which depicts *a weight that is heavy or crushing or a crushing weight*. It can refer to either *a physical problem, circumstantial problem*, or *spiritual problem*. Rather than being a typical, everyday burden, it is *a burden too heavy to carry alone*, such as a habitual sin that has plagued a person for years on end. If one attempts to carry a burden like this alone, it would be crushing to bear.

In this verse, Paul is teaching us that when we see someone that's under a heavy load, rather than just look at them in pity and say, "What you're going through must be so difficult," we are to fulfill the law of Christ and crawl under their load with them and help them carry it. That's what Jesus did for us when He carried the Cross and took our punishment upon Himself. He did it for us, and when we see someone struggling and we come alongside them and begin helping them shoulder their overwhelming burden, we fulfill the law of Christ.

A besetting sin in our lives isn't the only burden (*baros*) that can weigh us down. A pressing burden can also be something good and godly, such as a vision or dream God gives us in order to see His plans and purposes carried out on the earth. When we're carrying this kind of burden, our natural minds can't fathom how He will bring to pass what He has spoken to us. It is then that we realize we cannot carry out our divine assignment by ourselves.

Thankfully, when we are faced with this type of burden, God has promised to bring us "support from Zion" (*see* Psalm 20:2 *NIV*). This often includes Him bringing other brothers and sisters in Christ into our lives that not only encourage and refresh us, but also help us carry out the vision in natural, practical ways. Similarly, it will be your role at times to help others press on and overcome so their God-given dreams can come to pass. Ultimately, as we help bear each other's burdens, we will cause one another to become more and more dependent on Jesus, not each other, and get back on track with the Holy Spirit and be filled with the Word of God.

'Consider' and 'Provoke' One Another to Love and Good Works

Without question, God has provided the local church to the Body of Christ as the answer for the dream thief of isolation. This principle is made clear in Hebrews 10:24 and 25, which says:

> **And let us consider one another to provoke unto love and to good works: not forsaking the assembling of ourselves together, as the manner of some is; but exhorting one another: and so much the more, as ye see the day approaching.**

When the Bible says, "And let us consider one another," the word "consider" is the Greek word *katanoeo*, which is a compound of *kata* and *noeo*. The ward *kata* carries the idea of *something coming down hard* and is dominating and *subjugating*; and the word *noeo* means *to think*. When these words are joined to form *katanoeo*, it means *to thoroughly consider*. In a literal sense, it means *to think something through from the top to the bottom*; to *deeply ponder*. This word *katanoeo* pictures *a person engaged in focused and concentrated consideration*. Moreover, it presents the idea of *mulling something over* or *carefully contemplating*. We could also say it means *to ponder and carefully look at a particular issue* or *to examine and fully study a subject*.

In the context of Hebrews 10:24, when the writer says, "And let us consider one another," he is basically saying, *"Let us carefully examine and fully study one another."* When you study a person long enough, you begin to know what they're thinking without them saying a word. You can sense when they're afraid, angry, or discouraged and you know what to do to encourage them and help dispel their fears. The purpose of this thorough pondering is so that we can learn how "...to provoke [each other] unto love and to good works..." (v. 24).

In Greek, the word "provoke" is a translation of the word *paroxusmos*, a compound of the words *para* and *xusmos*. The word *para* means *to come alongside* and signifies being in relationship; and the word *xusmos* means *to stick, to poke,* or *to prick with a sharp instrument*. When these words are compounded to form *paroxusmos*, it is the picture of *being side by side in a relationship with someone, and you're poking, prodding, and pricking them to move in the right direction*.

In a negative sense, the word *paroxusmos* means *to call into combat; to irritate, to incite, to anger, to inflame,* or *to enrage.* A clear picture of *paroxusmos* used negatively is found in Acts 15 where Paul and Barnabas sharply disagreed over taking John Mark on their second missionary journey. The Bible says the contention between them was so *sharp,* they parted ways, and Paul chose Silas as his travel companion (*see* Acts 15:39,40). The word "sharp" in verse 39 is this same Greek word *paroxusmos,* which means Paul and Barnabas were *para* (alongside of each other), exchanging verbal jabs that provoked, incited, and enraged one another.

In Hebrews 10:24, however, the word *paroxusmos* — translated as "provoke" — is telling us that in our relationships, we should be prodding, poking, and inciting one another to "love and good works." We should be continually sharpening and encouraging each other not to quit and give up on our dream but to become better, stronger, and more like Jesus.

You Need the Daily Encouragement of Others

Another important reason to develop and nurture godly relationships is found in Hebrews 3:13, which says, "But exhort one another daily, while it is called To day; lest any of you be hardened through the deceitfulness of sin." This verse lets us know that we need encouragement *every single day.* The word "exhort" is the Greek word *parakaleo,* which was used to describe *a military commander or captain who came alongside his troops and encouraged them to hold their head high, throw their shoulders back, and march into battle bravely.*

In the same way, we need fellow believers in our lives who will come alongside us and say, "Hold your head high, throw your shoulders back, and keep moving forward with what God told you to do! Don't give up! You can do what He asked you to do!"

Friend, don't swallow the lie that doing life alone is the answer. Isolation leads to devastation. Make it your aim to share your life with other like-minded believers. Their passion for God and love for you will help keep your dreams fresh and alive and protect your heart from becoming hardened to the things of God. Daily fellowship will enable you to "...hold fast the profession of [your] faith without wavering; (for he is faithful that promised)" (Hebrews 10:23).

STUDY QUESTIONS

Study to shew thyself approved unto God, a workman that needeth not to be ashamed, rightly dividing the word of truth.
— 2 Timothy 2:15

1. In the beginning, after God created every plant, animal, and even the first human, He saw that it was *good*. According to Genesis 2:18-25, what was the first problem God saw on earth — *before* sin entered the world? How did He solve it? What does this tell you about the importance of community?

2. Most would agree that Moses was a phenomenal leader who was mightily used by God. But did you know that God sent people into his life to help bear the burden of leading the nation of Israel? Who were his helpers, and how did they make it possible for Moses to lead effectively without losing his sanity trying to fix everyone's problems? (*See* Exodus 17:8-13; 18:13-27; Numbers 11:10-17.) What does this example from Moses' life speak to you personally?

3. One of the most impactful friendships ever mentioned in Scripture is that of David and Jonathan. Their interaction is seen throughout First Samuel 18 through 20. How did Jonathan's friendship help preserve David's life and ensure that he made it to fulfill his destiny? (*See* First Samuel 20 and 23:15-18.) What does their relationship show you about the value of deep, godly friendships?

PRACTICAL APPLICATION

But be ye doers of the word, and not hearers only,
deceiving your own selves.
— James 1:22

1. Can you think of a person (or people) that God brought into your life at a crucial time when you needed it most? Who was it? What was burdening you at that time? How did they encourage and refresh your heart?

2. Now think about the season of life you're in currently. Who has God intentionally placed in your path for this season? How can you connect more intentionally with them?

3. If you've struggled with fear of connecting with people, ask God to help you find and take the right steps to build godly community with

other believers. Start to think about the qualities or strengths that you might need in a friend. What are they? Begin to pray for God to send you a godly friend (or friends) who have those traits. Look for these individuals to start showing up in your life. Remember, He's always ordering your steps, and He will show you what to do (*see* Proverbs 3:5-6; Isaiah 30:21; John 14:26; Psalm 32:8.)

4. Lastly, who is someone you know that God has placed in your life that *you* can be a blessing to? Write down whoever the Holy Spirit brings to mind. What gifts or strengths do you have that might be helpful to them? How might you encourage them in their faith and help them fulfill their dream?

LESSON 10

TOPIC

The Consequences of Surrender

SCRIPTURES

John 6:1-14 — After these things Jesus went over the sea of Galilee, which is the sea of Tiberias. And a great multitude followed him, because they saw his miracles which he did on them that were diseased. And Jesus went up into a mountain, and there he sat with his disciples. And the passover, a feast of the Jews, was nigh. When Jesus then lifted up his eyes, and saw a great company come unto him, he saith unto Philip, Whence shall we buy bread, that these may eat? And this he [Jesus] said to prove him: for he himself knew what he would do. Philip answered him, Two hundred pennyworth of bread is not sufficient for them, that every one of them may take a little. One of his disciples, Andrew, Simon Peter's brother, saith unto him, There is a lad here, which hath five barley loaves, and two small fishes: but what are they among so many? And Jesus said, Make the men sit down. Now there was much grass in the place. So the men sat down, in number about five thousand. And Jesus took the loaves; and when he had given thanks, he distributed to the disciples, and the disciples to them that were set down; and likewise of the fishes as much as they would. When they were filled, he said unto his disciples, Gather up the fragments that remain, that nothing be lost. Therefore they gathered them together, and filled twelve baskets with the fragments of the five barley loaves, which remained over and above unto them that had eaten. Then those men, when they had seen the miracle that Jesus did, said, This is of a truth that prophet that should come into the world.

GREEK WORDS

No Greek words were shown on the program.

SYNOPSIS

We all have crossroads in our lives — moments in time in which God speaks to our hearts, and we choose either to stand by the word of the Lord or to go our own way. These crossroads can seem great or small, but none of them lacks significance. Our lives today are nothing more than the result of the decisions we made yesterday and all our previous days.

The fact is, you are the "control center" of your life, and ultimately, if you don't fulfill your divine destiny, you can point your finger at no one else but yourself. Thus, the last dream thief we are going to examine is far more personal than any other, which makes it the most powerful and seductive of all. If you can overcome this one, you can do anything God will ever call you to do. This seventh dream thief is called *you*.

The emphasis of this lesson:

The boy with five loaves and two fish chose to entrust what he had into the hands of Jesus, and Jesus used it to bring God glory. Jesus will gladly receive whatever you place in His hands. If you withhold from Him what He is asking for, you and others will miss out on the amazing miracle He desires to do. But if you will overcome *you*, He will take what you give Him and pour something back into your life that is far beyond your wildest dreams.

A Massive Multitude Kept Following Jesus

On one occasion, Jesus had performed many miracles and supernatural signs — especially in and around the city of Capernaum. As the days passed, the crowds that followed Him grew greater and greater. The Bible says, "After these things Jesus went over the sea of Galilee, which is the sea of Tiberias. And a great multitude followed him, because they saw his miracles which he did on them that were diseased" (John 6:1,2).

Notice it says there was a "great multitude" that followed. In the Greek, this describes *an enormous multitude, which was massive in size*. Up until that moment, this was the largest crowd that had ever "followed" Jesus, and the Greek tense for this word "followed" indicates that *they kept following and following and following* Him. Why were they following Him so persistently? Verse 2 says, "…because they saw his miracles which he did on them that were diseased."

The word "saw" here is the Greek word *theoreo*, and it means *to watch act by act, like spectators watching a theatrical performance*. It is the same word for "theater." Interestingly, the tense of this word indicates ongoing action. That is, the massive crowd was *seeing* and *seeing* and *seeing* the miraculous power of Jesus on display as they continuously followed Him. The Bible says they saw the "miracles" Jesus "did." The word "miracles" is the Greek word *semeion*, which describes *miraculous events*, and the word "did" is the Greek word *poieo*, which means *to do; to make*; or *to create*. It is where we get the word "poet," and *it always carries the idea of creativity or creative action*.

Jesus wasn't just doing simple miracles like healing headaches or minor illnesses. The use of the word *poieo* indicates that He had a creative flair to His healing ministry. That is, He created eyes where there were no eyes, arms where there were no arms, and feet where there were no feet. He healed those who were "diseased," which is the Greek word *astheneo*, and it generally describes *a person frail in health*. It pictures *those who were feeble, fragile, faint, incapacitated, or disabled*. It can also mean *to be in financial need*. Jesus was supplying creative and supernatural solutions to unbearable situations like these.

The Events Played Out Like a Dramatic Performance

When we come to John 6:3, it says, "And Jesus went up into a mountain, and there he sat with his disciples." At the top of this particular mountain were large, grassy areas that overlooked the Sea of Galilee and a major roadway called the *Via Maris* — which means "the way of the sea," and it stretched from Cairo to Damascus. As Jesus and His disciples were heading to Jerusalem to celebrate the Passover, they left the crowded road, climbed the mountain, and found a place to rest and recline after many days of intense ministry.

Continuing in John 6:4, the Bible says, "And the passover, a feast of the Jews, was nigh." From where they were reclining, Jesus and His disciples could look down at the congested highway and watch all the people that were making the journey to Jerusalem for the feast. Apparently, at some point, someone in the crowd discovered that Jesus and His disciples had taken a detour up to the top of that mountain. So rather than just continue to Jerusalem, they all took the same detour and headed up the side of the mountain to see Jesus.

Verse 5 goes on to say, "When Jesus then lifted up his eyes, and saw a great company come unto him…" (John 6:5). The word "saw" is again a form of the Greek word *theaomai*, the word for a *theater*. The use of this word indicates that as Jesus was watching thousands and thousands of people leaving the highway to come see Him, it was like *a theatrical performance* playing out before His eyes.

And the Bible says they came "unto" Him. This word "unto" is the Greek word *pros*, which means *directly toward Him*. Thousands of people were moving *directly toward* Jesus, and He was concerned for their well-being. He knew they had to be hungry after the long trip, so He "…saith unto Philip, Whence shall we buy bread, that these may eat?" (John 6:5)

The word "buy" here is the Greek word for *a marketplace*, and if you read how the other gospel writers describe this event, they note that Jesus actually said, "Let's go to a local market and buy bread to feed these folks." Of course, this was a silly thing to say, and Jesus knew it. They were on top of a hill in the middle of nowhere with no markets around for miles. John 6:6 says, "And this he [Jesus] said to prove him: for he himself knew what he would do." Jesus knew what He was about to do, but He said this to "prove" or *test* Philip to reveal what he really believed about Jesus.

The fact is that the disciples had personally seen many mighty miracles of Jesus, including the wonders of Him walking on water, turning water into wine, and casting out devils. What they had *not* seen up to this point was a miraculous multiplication of food. They had a *deficiency* in their understanding of Jesus in this area. You would think that considering all they had seen, they would believe in faith that Jesus would come through just as He had done so many times previously. But they didn't. Instead of rushing to faith, they rushed to fear and began to panic.

What Exactly Were the Five Barley Loaves and Two Fish?

John 6:7 goes on to say, "Philip answered him, Two hundred pennyworth of bread is not sufficient for them, that every one of them may take a little." In Greek, a "pennyworth" is a denarius, and it equaled a man's pay for a day of work. The common wage in those days was one denarius for one day of work. Thus, 200 denarii were 200 days' worth of salary. Essentially, Philip said, "Even if we could gather 200 days of salary in this moment and buy bread, it wouldn't be enough for everyone to have a little." The word "little" is the Greek word *brachus*, which describes *something very small; a fragment*. Two hundred denarii of bread wouldn't have given each person *a fragment* of food to eat.

At that point, Scripture says, "One of his disciples, Andrew, Simon Peter's brother, saith unto him, There is a lad here, which hath five barley loaves, and two small fishes: but what are they among so many?" (John 6:8,9) It's interesting to note that the word "lad" is the Greek word *paidarion*, and it describes *a very young boy, probably between the age of five and seven*. This little fellow had brought a lunch of five barley loaves and two small fishes.

Now this may surprise you, but the Greek term for "barley loaves" — *artous krithinous* — describes *a fragile and inferior bread* or *a barley cracker*. Furthermore, the phrase "small fishes" is the Greek word *opsarion*, and it describes *a small fish about the size of a sardine or minnow, which was usually pickled or cooked*. So the "bread and fish" the boy had were not five loaves of bread and two normal-sized fish as you might have imagined. This little boy had two *minnows* to put on the five *barely crackers* to have for a snack.

More than likely, this child was traveling with his parents, and his mom had given him the crackers and fish as a snack to eat while they were traveling. When it seemed like the moment had finally arrived for him to reach into his pocket and retrieve his handful of food, suddenly a disciple showed up and said, "Hey! Don't eat that! The Master needs what you have in your hand." So they took the little boy to the top of the hill to Jesus.

It's important to reiterate that if 200 days of wages were not enough to give even a fragment of food to each of the people that were there, what good were five barley crackers and two minnows with such an enormous crowd?

The Miracle of Multiplication

John 6:10 then says, "And Jesus said, Make the men sit down. Now there was much grass in the place. So the men sat down, in number about five thousand." Interestingly, the word "men" in the Greek is *andros*, and it describes the men, *the fathers*, or *the heads of households*. The fact that this verse says that 5,000 men — *fathers* or the *heads of households* — sat down, we know that they were not alone. Their families were with them, and a typical Jewish family in those days was very large. In fact, it was not unusual for a Jewish family to have as many as ten children.

That said, it is safe to say that the estimated crowd that was with Jesus was somewhere around 40,000 or perhaps even 50,000 people. Yet, whether it was 5,000 or 50,000, five barley crackers and two minnows weren't going to feed the crowd — regardless of how small the pieces were cut. Although the disciples saw lack in this situation, Jesus saw opportunity — a chance to prove His miraculous power once again to His apostles in training and all those gathered.

Verse 11 says, "And Jesus took the loaves; and when he had given thanks, he distributed to the disciples, and the disciples to them that were set down; and likewise of the fishes as much as they would." The word "took" in this verse would better be translated as *received*. Jesus will never take anything from you, but He will gladly *receive* whatever you place in His hands and will use it for His glory. He'll receive you, your family, your business, your ministry, your finances — anything. This little boy willingly gave his five barley crackers and two minnows to Jesus, and once they were in His grasp, it says He had "given thanks." This is the Greek word *eucharisteo*, which describes *a free-flowing stream of thankfulness and gratitude*.

As gratefulness was flowing, Jesus began worshiping the Father as the great Provider. In that moment, something miraculous began to happen in His hands. As He "distributed" the barley crackers and minnows — which in Greek means *to divide* or *sever* — the food multiplied in His hands! The disciples kept coming and coming, and Jesus kept giving and giving — worshiping the Father all the while.

"When they were filled, he said unto his disciples, Gather up the fragments that remain, that nothing be lost" (John 6:12). The Greek tense here actually says, "When they were *double filled*." In other words, they ate like gluttons! These people kept eating and eating and eating until they could eat no more. Scripture goes on to say, "Therefore they gathered them together, and filled twelve baskets with the fragments of the five barley loaves, which remained over and above unto them that had eaten. Then those men, when they had seen the miracle that Jesus did, said, This is of a truth that prophet that should come into the world" (John 6:13,14).

Can you imagine the range of emotions the disciples experienced? They went from fearful panic in the beginning to shock and utter amazement at the end, having 12 basketfuls of food left over. How about the little boy? No one understood the immensity of the miracle quite like him. He knew the minuscule amount of food Jesus had to work with because he himself had placed it in Jesus's hands. If he had hidden his fish and crackers or eaten them to satisfy his hunger, he would have completely missed out on this amazing miracle at the hands of the Master.

So What's in Your Hands?

What do you have that God is asking you to entrust to Him? What is He asking you to release into His hands? Is it your job? Your finances? Certain friends? Whatever it is, if you will overcome *you* — your fleshly, carnal, unrenewed nature — He'll take what you give Him and pour something back into your life that is far beyond your wildest dreams.

When the Lord asked Rick to move his family to the former Soviet Union, he was like the boy with the five barley crackers and two minnows. Letting go and surrendering the ministry he and Denise had worked so hard to build was extremely difficult. But the Lord told him something that he just couldn't get out of his mind. He said, "Rick, you can stay where you are and keep doing what you're doing, and I'll bless it. But if you don't release to Me what I'm asking you to yield, you'll never know what I could have done with your life."

Friend, that is the same statement the Holy Spirit is saying to *you* today. You can stay where you are and keep doing what you're doing, but if you don't release to God what He's asking you to release, you'll never know what He could have done with your life. Don't listen to the voices of the dream thieves or let them steal from you another day. Surrender yourself and all that you have to Jesus. The consequences of such surrender are simply magnificent!

STUDY QUESTIONS

*Study to shew thyself approved unto God, a workman that
needeth not to be ashamed, rightly dividing the word of truth.*
— 2 Timothy 2:15

1. Having a literal, physical need for food to survive is an incredibly vulnerable position to be in, which is why Jesus' miraculous provision of the loaves and fishes touched the hearts of so many people. In what other ways did God provide much-needed food for His people in Old Testament times? (*See* Exodus 16; First Kings 17:1-16; Second Kings 4:1-7; 42-44.) What do these examples say to you about God's ability to provide for your basic needs?

2. Take another look at the original meaning of the words "barley loaves" and "two fishes." How do these more specific definitions expand your understanding of this passage and make the miraculous power of Jesus more profound?

3. Just like the little boy who was willing to give up his lunch to feed the crowds, Mary, the mother of Jesus was willing to surrender herself to God's plan for her life. According to Luke 1:26-45, how did she respond to God's call? What does her story tell you about the power of simply believing and being willing to surrender ourselves — our dreams, our resources, our plans — to God?

PRACTICAL APPLICATION

*But be ye doers of the word, and not hearers only,
deceiving your own selves.*
— James 1:22

Can you imagine being in that little boy's shoes? The truth is you are! God has blessed you with a number of "barley crackers and minnows." These include your time, talent, finances, and other gifts and resources, but when they remain in *your* hands alone, they stay small. However, when you place them in the hands of Jesus, He is able to miraculously multiply their reach and effectiveness. Stop and think:

1. *Is there anything in my possession that I'm withholding from God? If so, what is it?*

2. *What worry or fear (if any) is causing me to withhold these things?*
3. *Am I settling for much less than what God wants for my life?*

How does this lesson on the loaves and fishes encourage and motivate you to entrust God with what you have?

Notes

CLAIM YOUR FREE RESOURCE!

As a way of introducing you further to the teaching ministry of Rick Renner, we would like to send you free of charge his teaching CD, "How To Receive a Miraculous Touch From God."

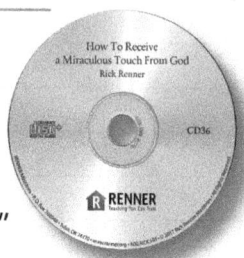

In His earthly ministry, Jesus commonly healed *all* who were sick of *all* their diseases. In this profound message, learn about the manifold dimensions of Christ's wisdom, goodness, power, and love toward all humanity who came to Him in faith with their needs.

☑ **YES, I want to receive Rick Renner's monthly teaching letter!**

Simply scan the QR code to claim this resource or go to: **renner.org/claim-your-free-offer**

Connect
WITH US!

www.ingramcontent.com/pod-product-compliance
Lightning Source LLC
Chambersburg PA
CBHW061457040426
42450CB00008B/1394